Footy Grounds to Grandstands

Sam Duncan

Footy Grounds to Grandstands

Play, Community and the
Australian Football League

Acknowledgements:

To my wife Sarah, to my mum and dad and family, to the footy fans whose views helped bring this book to life, and to my mentor and supporter, Arran Gare, thank you. I hope you all enjoy the read!

Footy Grounds to Grandstands: Play, Community and the Australian Football League
ISBN 978 1 76041 248 7
Copyright © Sam Duncan 2016
Cover photo by Mobilegnome, Sydney vs Essendon 2009

First published 2016 by
GINNINDERRA 6RESS
PO Box 3461 Port Adelaide 5015
www.ginninderrapress.com.au

Contents

Foreword		7
Introduction		9
1	Our Game, Our Communities	13
2	Play, Community and Culture	27
3	The Commodification of Play	39
4	The Play–Money–Media Cycle	52
5	The Transformation of the AFL	62
6	The Manipulation and Corruption of Play	81
7	Grassroots vs AFL Communities	97
8	From Communities to Markets	110
9	Members, Supporters and Fans: Views from the Grandstands	127
10	A Global Phenomenon	138
11	The AFL Today	144
12	Re-establishing Community	155
Notes		164
Bibliography		175
Appendix: AFL Fans Interviewed		186

Foreword

Australian Football has been transformed. AFL football today is a long way from the game's 1850s foundations. The AFL, the Mount Everest of the game, is far from local footy clubs today and the VFL clubs of even 40 years ago.

Recognising the passions of supporters of Australia's biggest spectator sport, Sam Duncan is aware of how the game has changed. He writes about the Mount Everest and about footy's Himalayas, the local leagues, the grass roots of football. He shows how footy is much more than its major role as a weekend escape from the workaday world as captured in 'Up There Cazaly'.

Sam Duncan writes about the best traditions of play which have always shaped the game. Play as experienced by AFL players, by kids having a kick to kick or at Auskick, by local footballers and by supporters at the game, and those following it on radio and television. Local footy and AFL supporters still maintain social traditions of community and of joy, as well as despair, in each game.

However, the field of play is also now shaped by the media field, through which the game is now transmitted, and by the fields of business. While their passions are central for many AFL supporters and even more for partisans of local football clubs, at the same time, players can be 'commodified' and members 'monetised', as part of club finances.

AFL clubs are often shaped by the KPIs, or key performance indicators, both on and off the field. At times, AFL matches are the product of players 'playing their roles' and 'keeping to our structures'. And with everyone packed inside one 50-metre line.

In this stimulating book, Sam Duncan explores the best traditions of the game in the spirit of play and community. He also explores footy as work and as business, the threat to footy's traditions from neoliberal economics which influence the AFL, its clubs and the media.

Like many a great match, *Footy Grounds to Grandstands* is also stimulating. It is a great read.

Stephen Alomes

Stephen Alomes, a sports and cultural historian at RMIT, is the author of *Australian Football The People's Game 1958–2008* (2012).

Introduction

Australian citizens have always shared a special relationship with sport. What is now often described as a national obsession began as a pastime for men and women who wanted to maintain a certain level of fitness or who enjoyed coming together with other citizens to participate in free and vigorous activity. Sport and sporting clubs spawned in the early days of Australian settlement and developed into cornerstones of their local communities. They served as a form of identity for citizens, one based on the games they played, the teams they followed and the passion citizens expressed through them. Indeed, these clubs were the spiritual homes of their communities.

In the last thirty years, however, elite-level sport has undergone an unprecedented rapid, almost universal, transformation. Professional sporting organisations around the world seem almost unrecognisable when compared with their earlier forms. No longer are professional athletes simply the best players in their sport; nor are professional sporting clubs simply the homes of hopes, dreams and community aspirations. They are no longer hubs of their communities or true representations of their supporters and members. They are now businesses which strive not only to win but also to profit. Indeed, most sporting organisations consider winning an essential element in making a profit.

These clubs are also an important part of the entertainment industry, a tool for athletes, coaches, administrators, sponsors and the media to make money. Athletes, coaches and administrators are some of society's most recognisable, powerful and wealthy citizens. Globally, many professional sport athletes are multimillionaires, employees of their clubs, and ambassadors or sponsors of corporate organisations and their products. They are celebrities for society to see, hear and read about through an unquenchable media.

In the beginning, Australian football reflected the people who played it, a new game created for a new nation far away from the rest of the world. The game required wide-ranging physical and mental attributes: fitness, skill, spontaneity, courage and daring. Players were bold and brave: ducking, weaving, chasing and tackling. They flew through the air for marks, waited to rove the ball at the front of the marking contest and kicked goals or stopped them. They played with instinct and flair.

Players represented their clubs, which represented their communities. Home grounds were in or around their home suburbs. Players often lived close enough to walk to the grounds without working up a sweat. Coaches guided their players, training them during the week and assigning the positions they were to play. They fired up their teams with fire and brimstone speeches that today seem more appropriate to the theatrical stage.

And after the games were played and the contests won or lost, players gathered with their communities to recall the moments that mattered. Heroes were celebrated and villains from the opposition were often embraced, sharing drinks and letting bygones be bygones.

Football clubs were defined by the cultures they created and the communities they formed, both within the boundary lines of the grounds they played on and within the walls of their sacred clubrooms. But it was the act of playing, or, for some, of watching others play, that brought people joy. People came together based on an understanding that the way they played reflected their club and its people. Because the game was part of their lives, people understood its nuances and complexities. Football provided a common understanding between players and fans. Whether they talked about the game or grabbed a football and went out for a kick, the game brought people together. From play came communities.

That's what Australian football was – indeed, that's what football remains in some suburban and grassroots clubs around the nation – but it seems in many instances that is no longer the case, especially at the elite, professional level of the Australian Football League (AFL). Football is no longer simply what the AFL's motto, *populo ludus populi*, suggests: 'the game of the people, for the people'. While many supporters maintain their passion for the game, neoliberal ideals increasingly dominate the AFL landscape. Football has become a business.

The AFL is now less about spontaneity and more about structure. The bottom line takes precedence. Winning is measured and analysed within an inch of its life, as is player performance. Players still need to be fit, skilful, courageous and daring. They still need to be spontaneous and creative. They still need flair. But they must also play their parts carefully, knowing when to reign themselves in. They must understand their roles, stay within the structures of the team and stick to their club's game plan. Doing so earns them praise. Taking a cavalier approach to game plans and tactics may result in being dropped from the team.

Play is also more contrived and organised – and more confusing. And, with confusion, comes distance. Sometimes we don't even recognise the game. Home games are no longer played on home grounds in our suburbs. They are actually away games, played at the Melbourne Cricket Ground, Etihad Stadium or some other centralised location in Australia. We no longer have communal club rooms in which to gather to discuss matters with other confused fans. And we question, whether consciously or unconsciously,

- Who are the players?
- Where are they from?
- Is the club listening to me?
- How do I become part of its community?
- If I pay my membership to support the boys, what do I get from them in return?
- Do they even care? Or are they more interested in contested possession stats, the plus one or the goals converted from turnovers?

Thus, as play within the AFL changes, the communities around the game become weaker.

Notions of AFL communities, fan culture and the game's commercialisation have been explored and written about by Australian historians and academics.[1] However, none of those studies explore the role of the play element in creating communities, nor do they consider the impact of play's transformation for fans and the game's communities.

This book is an examination of the important link between play, culture and community. In it, we explore why and how the play element in the AFL has changed. We also examine the relationship between play and community in the AFL. We hear not only from cultural historians, academics and theorists but also fans, supporters and members of AFL clubs to gain their insights and reactions to the changes in Australia's game. Ultimately, we illuminate the AFL's transformation from 'the game of the people for the people'[2] into a multibillion-dollar business that has left the people behind.

1

Our Game, Our Communities

Australians love their 'footy' – Australia.gov.au

Play, games and sport have had integral roles in shaping Australia. Linked to the formation, growth and vibrancy of Australian communities, sport has defined and shaped the culture of this country, our national identity and our evolving position on the world stage. Indeed, many Australian historians have observed that sport has shaped the Australian character, bringing 'a sense of shared Australianness'[1] and helping us to relate to our fellow citizens on both national and local levels. Others have linked sport to the very foundations of our nation, the Federation of Australia.[2] Indeed, since the early nineteenth century, play, games and sport have impacted democracy in Australia as citizens come together to participate in the games, events and sporting clubs they created and to enjoy the feelings of genuine ownership derived from those creations. One of the most important of these has been the creation and development of Australian football, Australia's indigenous game.

The roots of Australian football

Although varying theories exist about exactly where and when the first forms of football were played in Australia, it is generally accepted that Australian football became more organised and more prevalent in Victoria and, in particular in Melbourne, from 1858. Thomas Wentworth Wills published a letter in *Bell's Life in Victoria* on 10 July 1858, calling for a 'football club, a rifle club or other athletic pursuits' to keep cricketers fit, healthy, occupied and active during the winter months.[3] Nearly one month later, on 7 August 1858, approximately eighty men comprising two teams, Melbourne Grammar and Scotch College, played the first game of Australian football, umpired by Tom Wills. The game was played in the parklands surrounding the Melbourne Cricket Ground (MCG), with goal posts approximately 500 metres apart. To win, a team had to score twice. The teams played the game over three afternoons, stopping each day at dark. At the end of the third day, Scotch College had scored the one and only goal; but because of the rules, the match was deemed a draw.[4]

The rules continued to evolve based on the advice and guidance of players from both this game and other experimental games played in Melbourne and Tasmania in 1858. On 17 May 1859, Thomas Wills, William Hammersley, J.B. Thompson, Thomas Smith, J. Sewell, Alex Bruce and T. Buttersworth met at the Parade Hotel in East Melbourne to develop the Melbourne Football Club rules, the first set of rules for Australian football. These men distributed the rules widely to community groups, local hotels and individuals who quickly took to playing the game.[5]

According to some, when Wills proposed a pastime for cricketers to play during the winter months, he originally considered a form of rugby in keeping with his schooling in England. However, he felt that the offside rules in rugby were not suitable for players older than schoolboys or for the drier environmental conditions in Australia. Instead, he declared that Australians 'shall have a game of our own'.[6]

Cultural theorists have suggested that the indigenous game of marngrook[7] influenced Wills in his creation of Australian football and its rules. Marngrook was a football game Indigenous Australians played which involved 'large numbers of players punt-kicking and catching a stuffed ball'.[8] The earliest anecdotal account of marngrook was in 1841. William Thomas, a protector of Aborigines in Victoria, claimed that he witnessed a group of Aborigines playing the game east of Melbourne:

> The men and boys joyfully assemble when this game is to be played. One makes a ball of possum skin, somewhat elastic, but firm and strong… The players of this game do not throw the ball as a white man might do, but

drop it and at the same time kicks it with his foot, using the instep for this purpose… The tallest men have the best chance in this game… Some of them will leap as high as five feet from the ground to catch the ball. The person who secures the ball kicks it… This continues for hours and the natives never seem to tire of the exercise.[9]

Wills was raised in the Western District of Victoria, just outside Moyston, where he often played with Indigenous Australian children. According to Martin Flanagan, the Wills family was so close to the local Indigenous community that Tom became fluent in the local dialect.[10] Inspired by the game he had played as a child, Wills developed what became Australian football.[11] Furthermore, Jenny Hocking and Nell Reidy have demonstrated the historical evidence for the influence of Aboriginal sport on Wills.[12]

If the game did develop from the Indigenous game of marngrook, then Australian football is truly the native game of Australia. However, other sport historians have rejected these claims. Gillian Hibbins describes them as fanciful, an 'emotional belief' lacking 'any intellectual credibility'.[13] Instead, she contends that the inspiration for Australian football was an array of British games such as rugby and Irish football that evolved in the 1850s into a game appropriate for, and reflective of, the Australian character.

In truth, English school football (rugby), Irish football and marngrook may all have influenced the foundations of Australian football.

The rules

The first set of rules developed in 1859 stipulated the following:[14]
1. The distance between the goal posts shall be decided upon by the captains of the sides playing.
2. The captains on each side shall toss for choice of goal. The side losing the toss has the kick-off from the centre-point between the goals.
3. The goal must be kicked fairly between the posts without touching either of them or a portion of the person of any player of either side.
4. The game shall be played between the space of not more than 200 yards wide, the same to be measured equally on each side of the line

drawn through the centre of the two goals and two posts to be called the 'kick off points' shall be erected at a distance of 200 yards on each side of the goal posts at both ends and in a straight line with them.

5. In case the ball is kicked behind the goals, anyone of the side whose goal it is kicked, may bring it back 20 yards in front of any portion of the space between the kick-off posts and shall kick it as nearly as possible in the line of the opposition goal.
6. Any player catching the ball directly from the boot may call 'mark.' He then has a free kick. No players from the opposite side being allowed to come into the spot marked.
7. Tripping and pushing are both allowed but no hacking when any player is in rapid motion or in possession of the ball except for the case provided by rule 6.
8. The ball may only be taken in hand only when caught from the boot or on the hop. In no case shall it be lifted from the ground.
9. When the ball goes out of bounds (the same being indicated by a row of posts) it shall be brought back to the point where it crossed the boundary line and thrown in right angles with that line.
10. The ball while in play may under no circumstances be thrown.

These rules certainly reflect the Australian way of life in the 1850s gold rush era, particularly in Melbourne, as several historians have noted. Richard Cashman states that the rules were an expression of the 'brash self-confidence' and 'larrikinism' evident in Victoria in the 1850s.[15] Bill Murray notes that Australian football, in its make-up and rules, maintained a greater degree of spontaneity than most other football codes, enabling players to play with a flair and freedom not seen in games with more restrictive rules.[16] According to Margaret Lindsay, 'When bourgeois society organised male physicality for its particular purposes, Australia and Australian football somehow escaped… perhaps because of the off-centre immaturity of Australian capitalism at the time.'[17] She describes the image of Australian football as one of 'extraordinary grace and beauty as well as ferocity and determination. It is dangerously, beautifully wild – rollicking, rolling, airborne, swerving, twisting.'[18]

Indeed the game, like Australia itself, was young, free and still developing. In many of its aspects, football, and life, led to an unrefined, loose, sometimes brash carelessness. Even the ovals on which the games were played were without specific dimensions, and remain so even today, with some of the larger grounds twice the size of rugby and soccer pitches. The general consensus among those who played and watched the game was that if a ground was 'oval enough' and 'big enough,' they could play a game of Australian football.[19]

The people's game

The idea of the game being of and for the people is reflective of the rapid groundswell of support for the game from the grassroots in its earliest years.[20] However, just as not all Australians follow the game today, it is true that not all citizens gravitated towards or participated in, the game during its formative years.

Therefore, the expression 'the people' when referred to in relation to Australian football, is not necessarily a term that can be applied to all citizens or even those who follow the game. 'The people' are those who embrace the game and who, in return, are accepted by others within the Australian football community, thus giving them a stake in the game. The game's motto, *populi ludus populo*, meaning 'the game of the people, for the people', reflects the nature of the sport as it evolved from a common passion shared by many within the community.

That Australian football was almost completely free of cost was of great importance to its growth. Parks were the predominant locations for the grounds, enabling communities to enjoy playing and watching the game free of charge. This encouraged people to embrace the game even more. As Blainey notes, 'If a few pence had been charged for admission, football might not so quickly have become a sport for the people.'[21] Because of its grassroots founding, the game reflected the way of life, values and characteristics of 'the people', including women, who were as fanatical about the game as men were. They felt as much ownership of the game as men did, were included in the development of the game and related to the spirit in which the game was played.[22]

As the popularity of the game grew from the 1860s through the 1880s, the people's passion and enthusiasm spawned the formation of suburban clubs. Indeed, the rapid growth in Victoria mirrored the growth in suburban and regional settlements. Most football clubs were created as expressions of the people's spirit and culture. From the players and supporters to the colours, nicknames and mottos, these clubs were the results of grassroots efforts that represented the people in each club's community. Thus, football clubs became the home and central hub of communities, as the Essendon and North Melbourne football clubs clearly exemplified.

The Essendon Football Club

The Essendon Football Club was formed sometime between 1871 and 1873[23] by the McCrackens, a well-known brewery family which hosted a team of local junior players at their Ascot Vale property. As the owner of several city hotels, Robert McCracken was an integral part of the community. Because city hotels often served as meeting points for the locals in Melbourne, McCracken soon discovered the passion and enthusiasm the Essendon community had for Australian football. He then used his influence to establish a football club to represent his community. As founder, McCracken served as the first president of the Essendon Football Club; his son Alex was its first secretary.[24]

The club quickly became an important part of the community. Its first matches were played at Kent Street Oval in Ascot Vale, known by the locals as McCracken's Paddock. The matches were then moved to Flemington Hill and were played on the Essendon Cricket Ground. By playing their home games in and around the Essendon area, both players and supporters could walk to their local grounds and meet in the club rooms afterwards. There they discussed the day's football match as well as community matters unrelated to football.[25]

However, in 1881, James Taylor, the mayor of Essendon, declared the Essendon Cricket Ground was 'to be suitable only for the gentleman's game of cricket'.[26] This forced the Essendon Football Club to move to East Melbourne, a move the community met with hostility, believing their local team was being taken away from them. In fact, the move led to the creation of another Essendon football team in 1900, the Essendon As. This team played a lesser calibre of competition than the original team.

In 1922, the expansion of the Jolimont railway lines through the East Melbourne Cricket Ground meant the Essendon Football Club had to seek a new home once again. The Essendon City Council, which had forced the club to abandon the area some forty-one years earlier, offered the club £12,000 to return to Essendon and to play on the Essendon Cricket Oval, known as Windy Hill. With the money, the club upgraded the scoreboard, built a new grandstand for local supporters, re-fenced the oval and returned to the Essendon Cricket Ground in time for the 1922 season. The team continued to play their home games there until 1991.[27] Although its headquarters and training facilities remained at Windy Hill, in 1992, the team began playing its home games at the MCG, moving them to Etihad Stadium in 2000. At the end of the 2013 season, Essendon moved its headquarters from Windy Hill to a new state-of-the-art facility in Tullamarine, where the team now trains and prepares for matches each weekend.

Because the Essendon Football Club was based outside Essendon (the suburb) for more than forty years, the club's community transcended geographical boundaries. In his history of the Essendon Football Club, Mapleston notes that it was class and even religion that characterised the community.[28] Following their relocation back to Essendon, the club began to reflect its geographical locale, the class and faith of its members and even the culture that spawned from the social interactions and experience of its community.

Their nickname, the Bombers, reflected the close proximity of Windy Hill to the Essendon Aerodrome. The club motto, *saviter in modo, fortiter in re* ('gentle in manner, resolute in execution'), described the culture of the community as well as defining the way the team hoped to play.[29] The club also reflected the predominantly Protestant religious faith of its membership – a defining characteristic of the club's playing group, coaching staff, administration and supporter base.[30] Pennings also notes that Essendon was the preferred club for those who were involved in the law and 'had many other professionals such as doctors, clergymen, military men and bank officials in its ranks'.[31]

The North Melbourne Football Club
Members of the St Mary's Church of England Cricket Club founded the North Melbourne Football Club in 1869 to keep themselves fit over the winter months. Now officially known as the Kangaroos, the club is often referred to as the Shinboners, its first moniker. Although the origins of the name remain unknown, some historians suggest that it arose because some of the players targeted the shin bones of opposition players during matches. Others claim the name derived from the local butchers, who showed their support for the club by dressing their beef leg bones in the club colours of blue and white, which are the colours of the players' uniforms.[32] Regardless of the accuracy of these claims, both illustrate the way in which the club name reflects the culture either of the team and the way in which it plays or of its community and the way in which it supports its club.

Like the colours, the Shinboner spirit continues today.[33] As long-time official and supporter of the club Ron Joseph stated, 'The clubs with bigger memberships, their supporters only touch their colours, but at North we have the Shinboner spirit. North people can touch that spirit – they are the real Shinboners, they are the club.'[34]

The Victorian Football Association

The Victorian Football Association (VFA) was founded in 1877. The VFA included teams from Albert Park, Hotham, Inglewood, Melbourne, Rochester and St Kilda. Six of these VFA clubs were from country Victoria.[35] As the popularity of Australian football continued to grow, more teams entered the VFA and crowds flocked to watch their local teams play. In 1886, two undefeated teams competed in Melbourne at Albert Park Lake to claim honours as premiers in the VFA: Geelong and South Melbourne. Two trains brought thousands of supporters from

Geelong to watch the contest. A record crowd of 34,121 fans watched Geelong beat South Melbourne 4.19 to 1.5. Afterwards, jubilant Geelong fans lined Clarendon Street in South Melbourne to cheer their players as they departed for their home town.[36]

Australian football stimulated great joy for the people who came to play and watch the game. As such, the Australian football community quickly swelled to include thousands of Victorians, stimulating a culture that quickly became engrained in the city in which the game was born. The first official Australian football team in Australia, the Melbourne Football Club, attracted as many as 10,000 supporters for their matches. The popularity of the game continued to grow because of its unique ability to generate a collective spirit and support from citizens of all ages and genders. From 1969–70 onwards, it became the winter religion in other southern states, such as Tasmania, South Australia and Western Australia.

Even though the VFA continued to prosper, some of the senior VFA clubs became concerned with the unevenness of the competition. They proposed a breakaway league consisting of the best performing VFA clubs and other select clubs. Thus, on 2 October 1896, the representatives from six VFA clubs met at Buxton's Art Gallery in Collins Street, Melbourne, to form the Victorian Football League (VFL).

The Victorian Football League

At the start of the 1897 season, the VFL consisted of the Collingwood, Essendon, Fitzroy, Geelong, Melbourne and South Melbourne football clubs. Almost straight away, these teams invited Carlton and St Kilda to join. The eight teams brought with them a huge following, ensuring the continued growth of the game in Victoria. The community of the inner working-class suburb of Richmond created the Richmond Football Club in 1908 and entered the VFL along with University (which only lasted until 1914). Three more community clubs – Hawthorn, North Melbourne and Footscray – joined the league in 1925, expanding the competition to twelve Victorian teams (eleven suburban teams and one provincial team).[37]

The new professional league also revealed what has come to be at the heart of the decisions, structure and formula of Australian football, as Robin Grow notes in his historical account of Australian football: 'The major reason [for the formation of the VFL] could be summed up in one word: money.'[38] The VFL emphasised economic capital and business objectives. The clubs required economic capital to maintain and upgrade their training facilities, home grounds, clubrooms and social club facilities. Supporters paid a small fee to their clubs to attend matches. Players were also paid to play the game. As Grow notes, 'They commissioned grandstands to improve comfort for their members and borrowed heavily to build them; to service such loans they needed continuous large cash flow from the gate; to ensure the paying crowds kept coming, they had to have a well performed team on the field; to ensure they kept winning, they had to pay players…and so it went.'[39]

To recruit the most talented players, administrators had to raise the necessary funds, often relying upon the generous donations of wealthy businessmen in their communities who supported the clubs. Collingwood, for example, received generous donations from tote operator and sport entrepreneur John Wren throughout the 1940s and 1950s to lure the best available talent to Collingwood and to ensure the club had the most up-to-date facilities and resources at its disposal.[40] Likewise, the Melbourne Football Club benefited from the financial wealth of the Melbourne Cricket Club, of which it was an offshoot. This financial support established Melbourne as one of the most powerful clubs during the early years of competition.

The administration and governance of all VFL clubs reflected the business orientation of society to some extent. Small-business owners and influential businessmen governed the clubs within their communities as members of their boards of directors. In turn, they made financial donations to their clubs.[41]

However, generating economic capital was certainly not the dominating feature of the game it has since become. Even at the elite level, playing Australian football was considered more a paid hobby or pastime than a job. Playing was a means of being part of the community and of creating and developing the culture of the community. In the 1940s, the maximum player payment was fixed at £4–£5, about two-thirds of the basic wage in the wider community and insufficient to cover all of a player's living expenses.[42] Thus, all players were employed outside of playing football. Many players even missed some games due to their work commitments.

The twelve clubs of the VFL also brought with them a sense of tribalism and community. The loyalty of both supporters and players for their clubs was entrenched through generations of family support based on bonds and attachments with their communities and the ability to share in a pastime they all enjoyed. The teams trained and played in their communities on their own suburban grounds, forming strong attachments not only to their supporters but also to their grounds: 'They were places of secular worship where people gathered with other rabid devotees to spurn timid opposition on Saturdays and socialise during the week. For some it would be where their ashes would be scattered.'[43]

The clubrooms were the centrepieces of their communities, their social settings. They were sacred places, separate from the ordinary and real, with their own rules and regulations, places where different members of the broader community came together and connected.[44] These clubs helped stimulate the culture of the community, a culture in which doctors, teachers, tradesmen, government officials, managers, blue-collar workers, men, women and children gathered as one to enjoying play with each other.

Ultimately then, within the VFL, money was subordinate to the spirit, community and culture of the game. Even at the elite level, Australian football was not considered a brand, a product, a commodity or a form of entertainment. Players played for fun. However, that began to change over the next decades.

Given the dominance of the game in the Melbourne landscape, the league acknowledged its need to ensure a growing fan base. The VFL's first step beyond the outskirts of Melbourne came in 1952 with the initiation of National Day. Created to promote Australian football as Australia's game, the VFL had all six matches scheduled for that day played outside the teams' geographical homes. Instead, games were moved to the Sydney Cricket Ground, Brisbane Exhibition Ground, North Hobart Oval and Albury Sports Ground and to the Victorian country towns of Yallourn and Euroa.[45] In the late 1960s, to provide a level of independence and autonomy from the MCG, the VFL also proposed the building of a mega stadium, VFL Park, to hold up to 155,000 spectators. However, when the stadium finally opened in 1970, its capacity was a more modest 78,000.[46]

By the end of the decade, the VFL had made significant movement towards a self-sufficient business model that included rationalisation and centralisation of grounds. Continuing to promote the game outside its traditional base, the league scheduled a series of exhibition matches in foreign countries during the 1960s to lift the international profile of the league.[47] The game also received much exposure through the advent of television broadcasts of Australian football matches, which resulted in decisions and new rules designed to keep the game as interesting and entertaining for fans as possible:

- expansion of the finals series from four teams to five in 1972;
- introduction of a centre diamond, later changed to a square, to limit the number of players allowed around the centre bounce to four per team;
- the addition of a second field umpire in 1976; and
- the replacement of substitutions with unlimited interchanges in 1978.[48]

Fears of unequal competition also emerged during the 1970s. Between 1961 and 1967, nine different clubs had contested grand finals; but between 1972 and 1987, only six of the twelve VFL clubs (Carlton, Collingwood, Essendon, Hawthorn, North Melbourne and Richmond) played in grand finals.[49] While some clubs flourished, others languished. As clubs worked to adapt to increasing business and commercial demands, they battled to find willing sponsors, advertisers and members in a city saturated with sporting clubs all competing for corporate dollars. Thus, the VFL looked beyond Melbourne to reach new fans and to sell their products to new markets.

From the VFL to the AFL

The Victorian Football League took its first step toward the national stage by moving one of its teams out of Victoria in 1982: South Melbourne, declared financially unviable at the end of the 1981 season, was relocated to Sydney in New South Wales. Four years later, the VFL continued its expansion, commissioning two expansion teams, the West Coast Eagles in Western Australia and the Brisbane Bears in Queensland, which both played their first season in 1987. Introducing the Brisbane Bears was a particularly bold move in that Queensland was a non-traditional football state that historically preferred rugby and rugby league to Australian football. This move proved the determination of the VFL to reach new markets.

In the 1980s, the VFL introduced its equalisation policies to ensure equality between all competing teams and the survival of its clubs. Both were essential to maintaining Australian football as an entertaining, unpredictable product. Equalisation included the introduction of a salary cap in 1985[50] and the first national draft in 1986.[51]

In 1990, the VFL renamed itself the Australian Football League. A year later, the AFL expanded the competition to South Australia, introducing the Adelaide Crows. In 1995, the league granted Western Australia a second team, the Fremantle Dockers. Unable to maintain the required level of financial stability and viability for a stand-alone club in the AFL, the Fitzroy Football Club moved to Brisbane at the end of the 1996 season, merging with the Brisbane Bears. Port Adelaide Power joined the competition in 1997. However, the twenty-first century brought the AFL's boldest and possibly bravest moves. In 2011 and 2012, the league introduced the Gold Coast Suns and the Greater Western Sydney Giants, the seventeenth and eighteenth teams in the AFL, respectively.

The Bears, the Swans, the Suns and the Giants were fundamentally different in their make-up from the foundation clubs in Victoria and the newer clubs in Western and South Australia. Rather than being built from the uprising of the passion and spirit of their supporters or the playing group, these clubs were franchises built from the top down, based on the identification of a new market, a fresh group of consumers from whom the AFL could generate economic capital.[52] Rather than entering the competition based on the collective will and desire of their communities, these clubs entered as businesses, eager to sell their brands and styles of play to consumers as their preferred form of entertainment. In many ways, this shift from football as a pastime towards football as a business was merely a reflection of the economic landscape in Australia and, indeed, in most of the Western world. The expansion of the AFL into New South Wales and Queensland was based on economic rational principles: play is sold as entertainment and the community is first and foremost seen as consumers viewing the game as entertainment. Thus, from the first eight clubs in the VFL, the Australian Football League has grown into the biggest football code in Australia, the fourth most attended sport in the world and a multibillion-dollar industry.[53]

2

Play, Community and Culture

Play is older than culture. – Johan Huizinga

In its purest and original form, play is based on enjoyment and fun. It is being free and spontaneous, 'a discharge of superabundant vital energy' to seek the satisfaction of some imitative instinct.[1] Although having fun is at the core of the play element, play may indeed be serious when one is engaged in the act of playing, but only then. Johan Huizinga identifies four characteristics of play:[2]
1. Play is free; in fact, it is freedom.
2. Play is not ordinary or real.
3. Play is secluded and limited.
4. Play creates order, is order.

The first characteristic relates to Huizinga's initial assumption that players feel free when they are playing. They are bound by no restrictions other than, perhaps, their ability to carry out a skill or a level of fitness sufficient to play at a desired level of intensity. Play is a voluntary action, not an obligation. Play occurs during free time when players are not restricted by boundaries or time constraints. Therefore, play is also to be free of cost and financial reward. Players are not to be paid to play; nor are they to pay to play.

The second characteristic indicates play is distinct from real life. According to Huizinga, play is inferior to real life: 'The contest is largely devoid of purpose...the action begins and ends in itself and the outcome does not contribute to the necessary life processes of the group.'[3] Thus, play can only be serious during play. No matter how intense, passionate or serious a battle when playing, its importance in real life is minimal. The players are only playing. Fundamental to this characteristic is the assumption that play is autonomous from the rest of society and that players act autonomously from the roles, responsibilities and power they may have in other parts of their lives.

The third characteristic extends the second.[4] If play is separate from real or ordinary life, it is also limited in its locality and duration. Play, especially within games, cannot continue indefinitely; nor can the games be played wherever. Games such as Australian football are played on a particular type of field for a particular length of time. These restrictions of locality enhance the distinction between play and real life. Furthermore, because play is limited in its duration and locality, it creates a sense of certainty, not of what is going to happen when play commences (for that is based on spontaneity and creativity) but of when and where play will occur.

This sense of certainty underlies Huizinga's fourth characteristic of play: the play element and its secluded, limited environment create order within the play contest. Even though play is spontaneous and free, the rules of a game, the playing area on which it is played and the duration of play all bring order to the play element by ensuring that some things within the unpredictable realm of play are predictable. Thus, knowledge of what is being played and how to play brings a sense of order. This sense of order is again reflected in sporting clubs formed around play. These clubs are separate from the ordinary world: they have secrets and rules that distinguish them from the real world, which adds to a particular sense of belonging and charm from playing.

Based on these characteristics, then, Huizinga defines play as a free activity standing quite outside the consciousness of ordinary life. Although play is not serious, it absorbs players intensely and utterly. Play is an activity connected with no material interest and no profit is to be gained from it. It proceeds in an orderly manner according to fixed rules within its own proper boundaries of time and space. It creates the formation of social groupings, which tend to surround themselves with secrecy and to stress their difference from the common world by disguise or other means.[5] These social groupings reflect Australian football clubs that exist around the country today. The level of engagement within the sporting clubs, for both players and non-players, helps to bind communities. More important, such involvement enables citizens to engage actively with others in something in which they feel ownership, thereby assisting them to reach their full potential.

Huizinga also sees play as being completely autonomous from society.[6] Through play, citizens come together to express themselves by participating in a common, shared activity they enjoy. These experiences become the foundation not only of community but also of the culture within that community. The culture, in turn, stimulates and binds the community together. Play allows citizens to define their relationships and to own the principles, values and virtues that determine the spirit in which they play the game. Thus, these games are essentially games of the people.

Huizinga is not alone in this view. Other modernists, including Hegel and neo-Hegelian British idealists writing around the time of Australian Federation, share a similar view. They argue that the underlying cornerstone of a political community is the active participation of its members in pursuit of the common good and general will of the community for a common interest and common goal. The relationships between the members of the community are based on shared common values and principles[7] and the culture of the community is the binding force inherent in these relationships.[8] Thus, the play element and the games of the people create the community and culture within a society.

The concept of community and its importance for both individuals and society is intricate and complex. The play element of a society is at the heart of how that society forms and defines its community and culture. In coming together in a common, enjoyed activity, citizens begin to create a culture through play that ultimately stimulates and binds the community.[9] But what is community?

Community

Community is often related to the concept of social capital, which consists of the networks, connections and relationships required to achieve common, shared, positive outcomes. Jane Jacobs coined the term social capital in 1961 while writing about the social relationships formed within typical American neighbourhoods. She believes that social capital derives from the organic development of a neighbourhood and that the power and authority within any neighbourhood must be decentralised and shared by its participants rather than by governments, business, developers or bureaucracies.[10] In feeling empowered to make genuine, meaningful contributions to enrich the life of the community, people subsequently develop a bond and cohesion with their fellow neighbours based on the sense of trust and responsibility they share with each other. Trust and camaraderie are essential building blocks of social capital. When a neighbourhood acts as a self-sufficient, autonomous economy, its citizens act to satisfy each other's needs, wants and wishes. In doing so, the neighbourhood becomes a vibrant, diverse, efficient and productive hub of economic activity. When people feel genuine ownership of their neighbourhoods and responsibility for them, they are more likely to be participants actively engaging within the community rather than mere subjects. They form a sense of social solidarity with fellow members of the neighbourhood and act in concert to enrich life within the community. Because they feel that they can make a difference within their neighbourhood and enrich their lives and the lives of their neighbours, they also feel a sense of individual satisfaction and self-worth.

According to Robert Putnam, social capital is at the heart of citizens engaging with each other and developing voluntary associations which are the foundation of interaction and discussion between the citizens of any society. Thus, social capital is foundational to individuals' social lives.[11] More important, however, is his belief that social capital accumulated within these voluntary associations constitutes the essence of true democracy.[12] Moral obligations, norms and social values – the three components of social capital – are essential in sustaining strong democratic societies.[13]

To illustrate the importance of social capital in sustaining strong civic engagement, community and ultimately democracy, Putnam compares the results of the different government reforms of 1976–1977 in northern and southern Italy. The reforms succeeded in northern Italy where government power was decentralised and new local governments were created to encourage and foster collective citizen participation to effect change in their communities. By providing citizens a local voice and a means to be heard, the Italian government effectively encouraged citizens to participate within society, giving them the choice to either enrich or undermine their communities. This, in turn, fostered a sense of civic responsibility, trust, assistance and collaboration, resulting in a sense of self-worth and satisfaction. In contrast, in southern Italy, the same reforms resulted in 'the imposition of hierarchy and order of latent anarchy'.[14]

Putnam also believes trust and the sense of obligation one citizen feels towards another are fundamental to freedom and democracy. At the heart of forming voluntary associations, such as sport clubs, is the fostering of active, free participation within them. These associations facilitate communication between individuals, improving the flow of information to and from individuals and increase the trust each individual has in one another. As a result, the sense of obligation members feel towards each other to help achieve their collective goals also increases. This trust binds the community together and enables members to participate freely within the organisation.[15]

To illuminate this theory, we must attempt to understand what genuine community means. The theories of German sociologist Ferdinand Tönnies and his concepts of *Gemeinschaft* and *Gesellschaft* provide an essential insight into the transforming nature of communities and an understanding of what the 'ideal' community may be.

Tönnies argues that social ties can generally be categorised as emanating either from interactions based on personal social interactions, roles, values and beliefs (*Gemeinschaft*) or from interactions based on indirect interactions, impersonal roles and formal values and beliefs (*Gesellschaft*).[16] *Gemeinschaft* provides a platform for citizens to come together to enjoy a common way of life. Through experiencing the traditions, rituals and activities of *Gemeinschaft*, members form a sense of identity and close social ties to other members of the group.[17] These social bonds are often based upon emotional connections, a sense of loyalty or obligation and a sense of responsibility members have to each other to help achieve their common goal, which ultimately ties the community together. In describing *Gemeinschaft*, Tönnies refers to collective will, a common way of life, common beliefs, concentrated ties, frequent interaction, familiarity and emotional bonds. Thus, *Gemeinschaft* reflects the ideal genuine community, which is fundamentally characterised by these properties:

- dense and demanding ties and social attachments,
- ritual occasions,
- a sense of loyalty,
- a sense of belonging and meaning, and
- a collective will.

According to Tönnies, when social groups are both homogenous and, more importantly, autonomous, they are genuine. Thus, when the collective properties of *Gemeinschaft* exist together within a community, the community can indeed be described as pure, genuine and real.

Many sociologists insist that Tönnies romanticises about an unrealistic ideal. Some who have disaggregated his properties and characteristics of *Gemeinschaft* argue that although each property has a worthy place in characterising community, to consider that all can coexist together in modern times appears little more than fantasy.[18] Although the characteristics Tönnies associates with genuine community appear far from realistic, they can still be found, in some respect, in many communities today, including modern grassroots communities such as local football clubs. An analysis of these communities reveals far more than just a distant reflection of *Gemeinschaft*.

Ian Andrews discusses Tönnies's concepts of *Gemeinschaft* and *Gesellschaft* in considering the changing nature of community in the AFL. In his study he rightly outlines the complex nature of defining and conceptualising community. He notes that while many theorists have attempted to define the term, most basic conceptions of community clutter around the following:

- community as a geographical locale
- community as a social system
- community as a sense of identity and/or belonging
- community as an ideology.[19]

Importantly, Andrews warns against making clear distinctions between these four ideal community types, which, he states, can frequently overlap. As such, community can exist as a place, but also as a sense or experience.

Yet relating the concept of community to Australian football is complex. As Dave Nadel notes in his article 'What is a football community', the expression 'football community' means different things to different people.[20] Indeed, in his paper he never actually defines what he meant by the term. However, Nadel does discuss the notion of 'imagined communities', which is extensively expounded in by Benedict Anderson in *Imagined Communities: Reflections on the Origin and Spread of Nationalism*. For Anderson, the narrative developed from participating in the community (and the subsequent relationships formed from such participation) needs to be 'imagined'. Anderson believes that a community exists in the minds of its members and is therefore a cognitive and subjective phenomenon, not a physical structure or even a cognitive reality. Importantly, he argues that the 'imagined community' is no less genuine than the physical one.[21]

Furthermore, American social historian Thomas Bender defines community as 'a network of social relations marked by mutuality and emotional bonds'.[22] He stresses that community is an experience, not a place. This is supported by psychologists, McMillan and Chavis (1986) who discuss the notion of community as a psychological sense.[23]

A sense of community

The properties Tönnies uses to describe *Gemeinschaft* provide a clear basis for citizens to develop a distinct sense of community which, in turn, allows them to create their own identities and develop their unique personalities. Sense of community is a concept which focuses on the 'experience' of community rather than on its structure, formation, setting or any specific feature of community. This concept supports the idea that genuine community is one of the major bases of self-definition.[24]

In their 1986 essay, 'Sense of Community: A Definition and Theory', McMillan and Chavis[25] argue that an individual's sense of community refers to

- a sense of belonging to the community;
- a sense of finding individual and collective meaning from participating in the community;
- a sense of collectively being able to influence the decisions and actions of the community;
- development of a sense of identity through the community; and
- development of emotional connections to fellow members of the community, which stimulate a sense of obligation and responsibility to each other and a desire to help achieve the shared and common goals of the community.

Thus, attaining a sense of community is fundamentally important to a person's socialisation process.

People develop their potential and sense of meaning through first attaining a true sense of community. By actively participating in the community and engaging in its historically developed traditions and rituals, humans develop their individuality and sense of identity. They develop their abilities to think independently through reflecting upon the traditions and relationships within the community and deciding either to embrace or reject them. They also accept certain obligations and responsibilities, although how they act upon them may vary from person to person. Ultimately, for members of a social group to attain a true sense of community and therefore develop as individuals, the community must be genuine and autonomous. Anything less corrupts the socialisation process. People must also be free to participate in community life. Anything that restricts them or inhibits them from doing so also harms their development and socialisation. Therefore, a genuine community is one that enables its citizens to feel a true sense of community within an autonomous setting, allowing its members to

- come together to enjoy something in common with others;
- feel a sense of belonging and meaning;
- form strong, emotional ties with other members of the community;
- feel a sense of loyalty, obligation or responsibility to each other; and
- influence and actively contribute to the shared and common goals of the community.

Culture

From its founding, Australian football has reflected the characteristics of the Australian people. Team members played the game with spirit, passion, enthusiasm and a vibrancy that reflected their ownership of the game and their pride in representing their teams and communities. Founders and supporters genuinely felt a part of the game as well. Thus, the game quickly embedded itself in almost all forms of Australian culture.

The influence of the people's game is readily seen in various artefacts of Australian culture, reflections of its grassroots founding and its strong resonance within Australian communities. In the world of theatre, writers have penned several plays based on fictitious events, characters and themes relating to Australian football. Among them are *And the Big Men Fly* (1963), *Goodbye Ted* (1975), *The Club* (1977) and *The Royboys* (1987). *The Royboys* explores the threat of commercialisation for the game. The narrative is about a battling working-class family who barrack for the Fitzroy Football Club. Together, they struggle to save their club from being renamed Fitzaki and relocated to Japan.[26] In an episode of life imitating art, some ten years after the first performance of this play, the real Fitzroy Football Club, unable to meet its financial obligations, had to merge with Brisbane and relocate to that city.

In music, composers of popular songs, such as 'Up There Cazaly', 'One Day in September' and 'Aussie Rules I Thank You', have written about footballers, football events and football moments. Mainstream artists have also referenced Australian football in songs such as Paul Kelly's

'Leaps and Bounds', which describes the excitement of walking to the Melbourne Cricket Ground to watch a game of football at the beginning of the football season.

Likewise, characters in mainstream Australian TV dramas regularly reference Australian football to connect with their audiences or to express their fictional personalities, lifestyles and interests. These connections also mirror the reality of the workplace. 'Footy tipping', competitions in which workers nominate the teams they think will win the scheduled weekend games, is a weekly staple in office environments throughout Australia. Thus, Australian football provides a way for people on the job, whether white-collar or blue-collar, to forge connections.

Play and democracy

Towards the end of the nineteenth century, T.H. Green, the British idealist philosopher, inspired a new liberal or social liberal philosophy in arguing that true democracy can only exist when all members of a society are free to participate in their community.[27] For Green, pure freedom exists in the pursuit of the common good; and liberty means full participation in the life of the community. Thus, for a society to be truly democratic, its citizens need to be collectively active within the community.

Green's philosophy is an expansion of Hegel's argument that the state is responsible for fostering the ability of its members to reach their full potential.[28] According to Hegel, the state is a political community because it is a cultural community. Its constitution is grounded in a national culture. Its political institutions are deeply interwoven and interdependent with all other aspects of culture and, similarly, express the values of the national culture. Individuals identify with the state through participation within the community – for example, through play. If people do not find their worth or identity through their communities, then they seek to do so through conspicuous consumption. Thus, Hegel considers it the duty of the state to ensure that the market is directed at achieving the common good of the community.

Green argues for an active citizenship and a collective will oriented to the common good.[29] Through freely and collectively working for a common and enjoyed goal, individuals within society can reach their full potential. Like Hegel, Green proposes that the role of the state is not to market but to nurture freedom and to ensure citizens develop their full potential and function effectively within their community.

Idealists in Australia adopted, embraced and extended this theory, arguing the importance of community and active participation within it in achieving genuine democracy. What idealism meant to early Australia is most clearly evident in the work of Walter Murdoch, a social liberal who taught at The College, Warrnambool, before becoming professor of English and later chancellor of the University of Western Australia. In his best-selling book *The Australian Citizen: An Elementary Account of Civic Rights and Duties*, Murdoch argues that the state is responsible for allowing citizens to realise themselves by attaining a good which is common to themselves and other men by nurturing the community.[30]

Donald W. Winnicott, an English paediatrician and psychoanalyst, argues the importance of play in enabling citizens to be free to form culture and communities. He relates the play element to psychoanalysis, stating that patients cannot be completely open or honest or be their whole selves if they are not able to play: 'It is in playing and only playing, that the individual child or adult is able to be creative and use the whole personality and it is only in being creative that the individual discovers the self.'[31] Thus, people are only truly free when they are playing; when they are unrestricted, spontaneous and creative; when they are being their true selves. It is during this play when citizens come together in an autonomous, unrestricted environment that they are free to do or act as they please. The end result of what they do and how they act forms their culture.

Furthermore, through the autonomy of play, people can get to know and trust their environment and develop trust for others within the environment.[32] The autonomy of play allows players to feel completely free to be their whole selves, their creative selves, their spontaneous selves. In doing so, they form real and genuine relationships with fellow players. From these relationships, they form communities and culture.

Thus, community, which is the core of democracy and of the relationships citizens share with each other, begins with the act of playing, as shown in figure 1. If play and community are foundational to culture, freedom, individual development and democracy, any transformation of the play element – and any subsequent weakening of the community – has ongoing consequences for both the individual and democracy.

Figure 1. Relationship between play, community, freedom

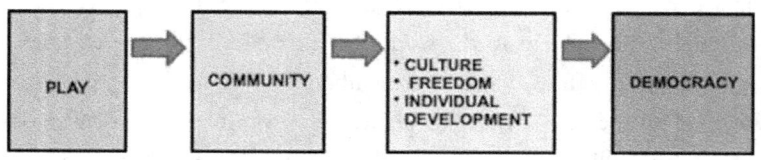

and individual development and democracy

3

The Commodification of Play

Australian football played at the elite level of the AFL has never been more popular or had a stronger presence in the Australian cultural landscape. However, since the early days of the Victorian Football League, the game has steadily been transformed from pure sport to big business. Before its ascension to the national stage, business entrepreneurs had not recognised the potential of the VFL as a means of generating profits. Neither had the media recognised it as a tool for attracting large numbers of consumers for hungry advertisers. Those views, along with the relationship between the game and the people began to change with the expansion of the VFL and its eventual transformation into the AFL. Today, the AFL is a several billion-dollar industry that reaches all states and territories of the nation and mirrors the capitalist and bureaucratic business model of Western and global civilisation. The rapid emergence of economic capital and commercialism in Australian football since the early 1980s also mirrors the dominant economic policies in Australian politics, economics and business.

The commercial boom and popularisation of Australian culture can be traced to the rise of neoliberalism in Australian political policy under Malcolm Fraser in the late 1970s and the Hawke and Keating governments beginning in 1983. According to Tom O'Regan, the deregulation of the finance sector, which enabled foreign financial institutions to enter the Australian financial markets and compete for customers, and the government's lifting of regulations on interest rates resulted in increased competition within the finance field. This competition ultimately led to a 1980s entrepreneurial boom that included the media and sport fields.[1]

Banks and other financial institutions became eager to lend money, fighting and bidding against each other to service bigger and bigger debts for increasingly indebted clients. As they lent millions upon millions to a new age of business entrepreneurs, these institutions turned to media advertising – and even sport – to sell their products.[2] Thus, the media had at its disposal a growing group of advertisers wanting to use their services to reach consumers. Because advertisers were willing to pay millions of dollars to reach mass audiences, the media increasingly looked towards sport to grow its audience and ensure continued advertising revenue. Thus, the relationship between sport, advertisers and the media resulted from the influence of money and the media in sport.

The AFL is seemingly managed according to the same principles and objectives as private organisations. Both the AFL and its eighteen clubs operate as businesses. Influenced by powerful, commercial, deregulated, privatised industries, the AFL has become a tool to generate profit. To do this, the league packages play, commodifies it, markets it and sells it. Thus, the league creates play from the top down, its once carefree, spontaneous, creative nature compromised by the neoliberal characteristics of efficiency, structure, team rules and set plays. By extension, rather than being owned by the people, play is consumed by the masses. Each individual and team performance is also reviewed, analysed and judged as a business judges its employees and their contributions to the bottom line. Thus, by measures of efficiency and effectiveness through a range of modern statistics, such as contested possessions, hardball gets, loose ball gets, inside 50s, clearances and other key performance indicators, clubs use similar principles, key performance indicators (KPIs), in their relentless pursuit to be the best both on and off the field as the private sector does in its relentless drive for profits.

Fields

To understand how the play element has been commodified, we must briefly examine the concept of fields and their interrelationships. Pierre Bourdieu developed a theory of field, capital and habitus to understand how citizens relate to each other and why they behave as they do.³ A field is simply any structure of social relations. In most societies, the major fields include the arts, education, law, politics and the economy. Although each field is generally autonomous and independent of the influences and characteristics of other fields, the economic field is the most dominant, powerful and influential to the point of minimising the autonomy of the other fields.

Capital is any recognised form of power that allows citizens to participate in a given field to gain further capital, thereby augmenting their positions within that field. Bourdieu identified four types of capital:[4]

- social capital: resources based on group membership, relationships, networks or influence and support;
- cultural capital: non-financial social assets that promote social mobility beyond economic means (for example, knowledge, skills, education and advantages) that give a person a higher status in society;
- symbolic capital: resources available to an individual on the basis of honour, prestige or recognition; and
- economic capital: command over economic resources, for example, cash and financial assets.

Habitus refers to a system of dispositions individuals develop in response to the objective conditions of a given field. Actors within any field gain capital and power as a result of their habitus, often constrained by the dominant characteristics of their surroundings. However, an individual's habitus also augments and reproduces the characteristics of the field. Having absorbed objective social structures into a personal set of dispositions, the subjective nature of an individual's actions reinforces the characteristics of the field and the relationships within it.[5] Thus, the behaviour of citizens and the relationships they share with each other are reflective of their environments and simply serve to legitimise and reinforce the existing structure of their surroundings.

Bourdieu argues that the limited characteristics of the field in which citizens are a part constrain their struggle for power. This struggle for capital also serves to augment and reproduce the existing dominant structure of the field.[6] However, when a field loses its autonomy to another more dominant field, such as the economic field, the struggle for capital changes to reflect the limitations of the dominant field. Citizens increasingly battle for the most dominant forms of capital which, in turn, further augment and change the structure and characteristics of the field. He argues further that when the economic field merges with almost any of the other fields of society, each field begins to mirror the other, as does the struggle for capital within each field.[7]

In terms of sport and the commodification of play, then, when the field of sport is autonomous, play is foundational to the culture, relationships and habitus of the field. Play shapes the characteristics, culture and spirit of its communities as evidenced by the formation of sport clubs in the early days of Australian football. In other words, the culture of the club is founded in the way its members play.

However, when the sport field loses its autonomy to other fields – that is, economic and media fields – this process is disrupted. The pursuit of economic capital begins to dominate the actions of those participating within the field. The struggle for economic capital characterises the culture, spirit and relationships formed within the field. This ultimately corrupts play and weakens the community.

At its founding, play in the VFL was almost completely autonomous from the economic and media fields. Money was required primarily for the upkeep of training facilities, the football grounds upon which teams played and the clubrooms where the community met to enjoy the game together. Some level of game promotion also occurred to inform communities of when and where their teams were playing and of upcoming club social events. Today, the relationship between play and the economic and media fields is far different, as shown in figure 2. Play is no longer foundational to the culture and spirit of the football club. Instead, the dominant neoliberal and business characteristics of the club determine (or corrupt) play. This is quite evident when we look at the influence of the economic and media fields.

Figure 2. Current relationships between the economic, media and sport (play) fields

The influence of the economic field

The dominance of the economic field in sport is particularly significant. In merging, sport has lost its autonomy, resulting in the subversion of the characteristics of play to economics. Measurements of statistics, structures of sporting clubs, team tactics and player instructions – all in the pursuit of success – now characterise the sport field, which has become a business.

Not only has this dominance changed the very definition of the play element, it has also affected community, culture and democracy. When sport was autonomous, players came together to play with spontaneity and flair, free of the restrictions and constraints of ordinary and real life. In being free, individuals could be their whole selves and, therefore, develop meaningful relationships based upon citizens coming together to enjoy something in common. This enabled citizens to form communities and define their culture.[8] However, since effectively merging with the rest of society, play is no longer autonomous or separate from the ordinary and real. Players no longer play with the same degree of flair, freedom and spontaneity because coaches and managers train them to perform in accordance with team rules, tactics, plans and structures. Performance is analysed for efficiency and effectiveness, resulting in a range of statistics reflective of any business performance review. As Stuart Osbourne, a member of the Essendon Football Club, notes concerning changes in his own club,

In the 1980s, they [players] were going to training two nights a week and playing a game on Saturday and going out for a few cans after the game. So, basically, you've got full-time footballers and full-time departments. I mean ten years ago, there weren't even football departments. You had a coach and a few runners or trainers or whatever and a doctor, of course. But these days, it's just a function of the professionals…which comes back to the money that's come into the game…players are [now] full time and they're surrounded by full-time support staff because there's so much money in the game.[9]

Alanna Ford, who barracks for the Carlton Football Club, concurs:

Every aspect of the game has been commercialised which in some respects has allowed the game to flourish…but it has also resulted in the demise of the tribalism of the game… The AFL is now as much about money as it is about the game.[10]

Thus, the constraints of economics and neoliberalism now define the dispositions of players, clubs and supporters. Financial contracts are the basis of relationships between players and their clubs. Financial memberships define fan support for their clubs. Economic capital determines the performance of individual players and teams.

The influence of the media field

The merger of the sport field with the media field has further affected the actions and decisions of key stakeholders, the play element and community. The media have transformed play into display, ensuring its use as a product to be marketed and sold to a mass consumer audience for profit. As consumers of the play product, fans have effectively defined their relationship with play through the market. Consuming entertainment with friends at a football match is far different from coming together to enjoy something which one genuinely owns or has helped create from the grass roots. Because the relationship individuals share with play as defined through the market is neither genuine nor real, today's communities are somewhat weaker than they were in the early days of Australian football.[11] The gambling industry links all three fields. Large national and international sports betting companies utilise the AFL to attract gamblers who want to place bets on a range of outcomes, including the winner, the margin and which player will kick the most goals in the game. Furthermore, while betting companies use the game as a tool to encourage fans to engage with their product, they also utilise the AFL as an advertising vehicle to promote their brand and their odds to the masses; match odds are often promoted during the game's TV and radio broadcasts. Thus, the play element is utilised by sports betting agencies to help sell their product, the AFL is utilised as a vehicle to advertise and reach prospective gamblers, and making money is the main game for betting agencies and gamblers alike.

Commodification and culture

As already stated, at the heart of Huizinga's definition of play are two beliefs:
1. Play is separate from ordinary or real life.
2. Players act freely, naturally developing a spirit and culture that define the values and principles of the community.

However, Huizinga notes that during the eighteenth and nineteenth centuries, play lost its autonomy to the all-encompassing economic market and subsequently to the media and entertainment industries. This affected both the play element and its relationship with culture. In this critical view, by the end of the nineteenth century, play was no longer free, no longer separate from the real or ordinary and no longer autonomous. As a result, play no longer determined culture. Instead, play forms had been transformed into commodities and were merely part of the culture industry, tools used to produce further economic capital.[12]

The origins of this transformation, however, were paralleled in an earlier time – the Roman Empire, a time when play was as much about those watching play as about those participating in play. The Romans organised and treated play as a tool to entertain crowds of keen, interested onlookers.[13] Thousands of spectators packed stadiums such as the Colosseum to watch contests or performances. According to Huizinga, with such use, play lost its innocence and was incorporated into the entertainment industry, its purpose transformed from creating community to amusing those who watched.[14]

Huizinga also argues that this move from play to display was a deliberate attempt by the ruling class to distract the proletariat from their otherwise subordinated and 'dull existence'.[15] Play was an item of escapism to keep the masses at bay and to engrain the position of the ruling class at the top of the social hierarchy. Thus, play lost its autonomy and became a commodity, an organised product of entertainment used to achieve a secondary result: escapism or reward.

During the Industrial Revolution, play lost its autonomy to the burgeoning business class and the bureaucratic model that gained momentum in Britain. Throughout industrialisation, games that included rough play or physicality were considered too unstructured in both rules and time. Such games often caused injury and, sometimes, death. Ruling elites became concerned with this behaviour; they believed that able-bodied men should compete in purposeful sport during their leisure time. Therefore, they made a more conscious effort to structure and organise play.[16]

Around this time, a moral panic emerged concerning the leisure-time activities of the working class; and pressure for greater control over working-class activities increased. Because workers were expected to arrive at work fit, healthy and ready for arduous, demanding shifts, some unorganised games were banned. To promote healthy physical activity and to remove unhealthy urges among working citizens, the ruling class organised sporting events. These activities ensured their workers were controlled during their leisure time yet could avail themselves of an escape so they returned from their leisure time content and ready to work. They also ensured that their workers were healthy and fit. If a nation's citizens were healthy, they were more likely to be productive and efficient in the workplace.[17] Sport helped to create character. Such were the beginnings of organised sport.

Money also played an important role in the emergence of organised sport. For the emergent entrepreneurial capitalist class who accumulated wealth by making and selling goods and services and for the working class who had no means of support other than their own labour power, the idea of professionalising sport and playing for pay held great attraction. Thus, pure amateurism in sport quickly died as entrepreneurs, capitalists and workers alike meshed to transform sport into a business in which all involved could generate profits and income.

As it became organised and structured, play transformed into sport and increasingly took on characteristics of serious business:

> What we are concerned with here is the transition from occasional amusement to the system of organised clubs and matches... Ever since the last quarter of the nineteenth century, games, in the guise of sport, have been taken more and more seriously.[18]

In losing its autonomy to the influence of money, play was no longer separate from the real and ordinary world. It was no longer free and, in many instances, had lost an element of enjoyment and fun:

> The spirit of the professional is no longer the true play spirit; it is lacking its spontaneity and carelessness. For the professional, playing is no longer just play. It is also work.[19]

Play became serious because play had been incorporated into the economic market. Play became a commodity, a skill, an item of labour, a shadow of what play was at its origin. Therefore, its role in society and in stimulating culture was reversed. Play no longer acted as the stimulus for creating the culture of a community.[20] Instead, civilisation, particularly the dominant bureaucratic business model of its time, determined play.

In the late 1970s, Christopher Lasch argued that we can no longer discuss sport and play as being beyond real and ordinary life. Corrupted by money, all play forms within society (both in leisure time and at work) have been superseded by individualism and the necessary calculation, prudence, analysis and efficiency to accumulate economic capital. Because the dominant bureaucratic business model that shapes modern society does not allow for pure play, citizens must increasingly turn to modern sport for their nourishment of play. Thus, they seek forms of freedom and spontaneity outside their ordinary lives through the leisure industry.[21]

Yet sport mirrors the very bureaucratic business model citizens seek to escape. Like business, sport is restricted by structure, analysis and a desire for success or for not failing. It is careful and concerned with its image. It is hierarchical, with management and coaches calling the shots, not the players. Sport is, in fact, now part of the bureaucratic business model. Because sport mirrors the neoliberal make-up of the rest of society, citizens cannot see that sport – and, within that, play – is no longer free, no longer completely spontaneous or separate from the ordinary or the real. It is a business, a part of the entertainment industry. Players are entertainers who display their talents for consumers. Thus, the act of playing at the elite and professional levels of sport is the players' work.

According to Lasch, the first stage of play becoming an object of mass consumption began as early as 1878 in the United States with the establishment of big time athletes in universities. In their quest for recognition and their desire to be better than their competitors, universities used sport, athletes and winning records to promote their brands and academic courses. Sport was also the tool for attracting enrolments and gaining financial support from local businesses. During this period, universities ceased functioning solely as universities and, like sport, began functioning as businesses.[22]

With all that, came the 'need to maintain a winning record: a new concern with system, efficiency and the elimination of risk'[23] to impress potential students and businesses which had invested in university programs. A new emphasis on drill, discipline and teamwork became central to play. Records and analyses arose from management's attempts to reduce winning and thus play, to a routine measure of efficiency. Management decided how a player should play. Structures were introduced, tactics were analysed and the inspirational appeals of old-fashioned coaches were met with amused cynicism.

Lasch bemoans the role of money in play, particularly at the expense of loyalty, stating that 'the athlete, as a professional athlete, seeks above all to further his own interest and willingly sells his services to the highest bidder'.[24] He also believes the sense of community from play disintegrated. What did exist seemed either fake or secondary to the individual interests and financial wants of the players, who increasingly saw themselves as entertainers in a show. However, these entertainers no longer played with the same sense of carelessness, abandon and spontaneity that had originally defined play. Instead, they 'performed' within a team structure according to a game plan using specific tactics. Their performance was then analysed for key performance indicators and efficiency. Thus, the prudence, caution and calculation so prominent in everyday life shaped sport as they shaped everything else.[25]

This era also introduced a new form of journalism, one which sold sensationalism instead of news. Such journalism helped to professionalise amateur athletes, assimilate sport to promotion and turn professional athletes into entertainers. Newspapers reported the business side of play, stories about clubs and their finances, in the sport section.[26] Thus, it was difficult to tell where play finished and non-play began.[27]

Commodification, community and democracy

If play once enabled citizens to form communities by coming together in a common, enjoyed activity that was autonomous and separate from other parts of society, then the commodification of play changed the dynamic of the community and the way in which the community is formed and defined. Thomas Frank argues the significance of this change in his book on the American financial industry, *One Market under God: Extreme Capitalism, Market Populism and the End of Economic Democracy*, stating that today's definition of community is largely based on individual interests and that money is at the core of an individual's freedom within a community. With money now underlying the foundation and the building blocks of community, the financial industry has become the model for this new form of community, encouraging mass participation. Thus, for the millions of people playing the stock exchange, the market represents them and acts in their interests and on their behalf. For them, playing the stock exchange mirrors the same notions of community and democracy Australia committed to at its founding: active participation, in common with others, as a community.[28]

However, this type of community is not real. Playing the stock exchange is based on the potential to accumulate economic capital. Participation is based more on individualism than on a collective good. Thus, playing the stock exchange promotes and justifies neoliberal ideals of free trade, privatisation, deregulation and individualism. Furthermore, even though participants may do well economically, their freedom becomes increasingly dependent upon their economic capital: how much they can accumulate and how much they can then consume.[29]

Thus, society, including sport, increasingly places making profit at the forefront of its operation and decision making. The extensiveness of this in sport has commodified the play element. Players make money from playing. Spectators pay money to watch players display their talents and now gamble on football. Media outlets reap millions from broadcasting play as a form of entertainment. Thus, although communities still exist in some way through participating in play, money now underlies their existence.

The consequences of commodification

Play can be spontaneous and creative when it is free from objectives or outcomes concerned with real life or when it is inhibited by the fear of real life outcomes, for the outcome only matters within the sport field. Only when we can throw off the constraints and burdens of real life can we leave behind our real life roles, responsibilities and limitations and fully embrace the environment of the autonomous sport field. When we are unrestricted or uninhibited, we are free to be spontaneous and to give our full selves when playing. According to Viola Spolin,

> In spontaneity, personal freedom is released and the total person, physically, intellectually and intuitively, is awakened. This causes enough excitation for the student to transcend himself or herself – he or she is freed to go out into the environment, to explore, adventure and face all dangers unafraid… Every part of the person functions together as a working unit, one small organic whole within the larger organic whole of the agreed environment which is the game structure.[30]

Thus, play is fun and free. Its spontaneous creativity arises when we throw off the constraints of real life and when real life does not influence play.

However, once the boundaries become blurred between the sport field and other fields of society, the outcome of play can have real life consequences. Because the play element is then no longer completely free from real life constraints, we are no longer completely free. When play loses its autonomy, the community no longer owns play and the prevailing values of playing. Instead, the culture industry owns and sells it to consumers. The values of play mirror those of the business model in the capitalist world; and the relationships consumers share with play and with each other become increasingly determined by their consumption of sport, based on the ideals, values and principles imposed by the culture industry.[31]

According to Jean Baudrillard's theory of simulacra, sport is the operational double of play. Baudrillard believes society has replaced all reality with symbols and signs, making all human experience a simulation of reality. Thus everything is in some way an imitation of something else, an 'operational double' that 'provides all the signs of the real and short circuits all its vicissitudes'.[32] As the operational double of play, sport is viewed as play; but, although its characteristics are similar to those of play, sport is not real play. It is merely a model of what play was, the symbols and signs of play. Because the structure, regimentation and controlled make-up of organised sport mirror the neoliberal business model that encapsulates most, if not all, of popular culture, we do not recognise that the play we see on the field today is not real, that it is not what play was originally. Even though moments of carelessness, spontaneity and bursts of energy make it easy for us to believe that play, in its original form, still exists, play is no longer free, no longer autonomous and no longer real because money now underlies play and its consumption.

4

The Play–Money–Media Cycle

It's the age-old sort of thing. I mean, eyeballs mean dollars…it means ratings; it means dollars. I mean, it's a pretty simple business equation. – Phil Wild, member, Sydney Swans Football Club

The media stranglehold on the play element has commodified play, packaging it as a form of entertainment that competes for the hearts and minds of Australian consumers, a tool used by the media to generate economic capital. Thus, almost all decisions made in the AFL are based in some way on the play–money–media cycle (figure 3) and the financial outcomes it offers all relevant stakeholders.

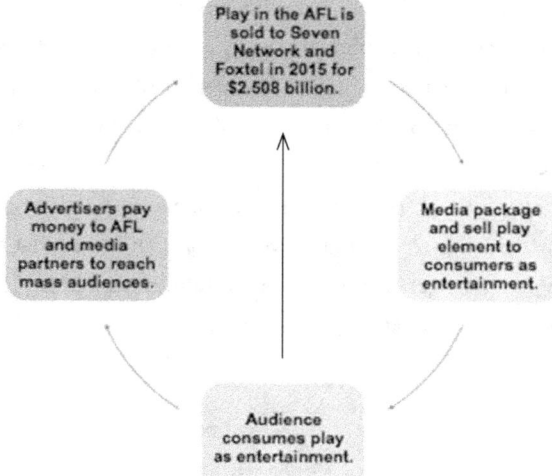

Figure 3. The play–money–media cycle resulting from the interrelationships between the economic, media and sport fields

Media interest in the AFL is almost like that of no other industry (sport or otherwise) in the world. Australian football has moved from a seasonal pursuit to year-round coverage. In 2015, the Seven Network, along with pay television company Foxtel, paid a record $2.508 billion to the AFL for exclusive rights to televise AFL play.[1] The average television audience for AFL matches during the 2015 season was 4.466 million per week. An average of 1.152 million tuned in to radio broadcasts each week of the AFL Premiership season, while over 46,000 listened through the official AFL App. Over 3.53 million Australians tuned in to watch the 2015 grand final between Hawthorn and West Coast. In addition, the AFL's online network attracted over 93 million visits during the 2015 season.[2] In 2010, the Seven Network accumulated an estimated $1 million for every five minutes of advertising during the AFL grand final replay, with one thirty-second national advertisement costing more than $150,000. The national TV audience for the 2016 grand final was 4.089 million.[3]

For the television networks, the high ratings of the grand final have escalated advertising revenues as advertisers capture a mass audience they can persuade to purchase their products.[4] Newspapers have also continued to fill their publications with stories about the AFL outside the regular football season to increase sales figures.[5]

But advertising is certainly not restricted to television, radio, newspaper, the Internet and digital and social media. The AFL and its clubs and collateral are also effective tools for reaching mass markets:

- Most grounds are named after their corporate partners.
- All clubs have major sponsors who advertise their logos on the playing jumpers or shorts of the team with which they partner.
- AFL finals series, award ceremonies and training venues are sponsored by corporate organisations, which are rewarded with naming rights.
- Companies sponsor players, benefiting from these individuals' popularity as performers.

Commercial organisations generally believe that by sponsoring leagues, teams, events and players they can increase awareness of their company brands and products or services and improve the images of their brands simultaneously. As Kate Withers, a Geelong Cats supporter, notes, 'When I'm at the game...[I'm] bombarded by visuals of advertising and sponsorship.'[6]

Sponsorship in sport also provides a vehicle for companies to reach new demographics or audiences while ensuring revenue for the AFL. Fundamental to this relationship are the media:

> Media coverage is often the most crucial single element within the reasons for a company entering into a sponsorship and it is certainly the one into which most effort must be put if you are going to ensure successful and continued results.[7]

To maximise their return on this investment, the media have ultimately packaged, marketed and sold the game as entertainment to as many consumers as possible. More consumers attract advertising demand and revenue, which increases media revenues and profit.

This play–money–media cycle not only favours media broadcasters and advertisers, but it also works to ensure the AFL and its clubs and players increasingly develop business and market characteristics. Furthermore, the cycle sustains itself because the AFL generates the money it needs and desires through its relationship with the media. The cycle also mirrors and justifies the bureaucratic business model of the broader society of which it is part. As Essendon supporter Zak Kardachi observes, AFL football 'sells because it just sells...no matter what'.[8]

The play-to-display transformation

One of the major impacts of the play–money–media cycle has been the commodification of the play element into entertainment. Traditionally, the most enthusiastic followers of Australian football, mostly men and women in Australia's southern, central and western states, consume the AFL through the media. Recognising the need to compete with other forms of entertainment and the potential of the game to resonate with previously untapped demographics and markets, the AFL and the media have sought to increase the appeal of the game in Australia's northern markets. For the AFL, the incentive is larger crowds and more consumers for their product to increase their income and bargaining power with media broadcasters. For the media, the incentive is equally simple: increased audiences transfer quickly into higher advertising revenues.

To provide advertisers with more varied audiences, the media ultimately have had to transform play into an entertainment package that men, women, children and families can watch and enjoy. With this philosophy at the forefront of their minds, the media have manipulated the game, transforming play into display. Thus, the broadcast of the game – and, thus, the game itself – has become a show. John Goldlust refers to this process as the transformation of play into display:

> To make match-day broadcasts as popular and appealing as possible, the media added many new entertainment devices. Pretaped interviews, live interviews during the match, background music, emotive colour pieces, close-up shots of the players and crowd, slow-motion replays, graphics, symbols and statistics all became part of the television play package in the AFL.[9]

As an extension of this, AFL play has increasingly become a regular part of television scheduling.

One of the more interesting consequences of the play-to-display transformation has been the changing role of commentators in these broadcasts. Once describers of what was happening on the field of play, commentators have become entertainers and promoters of the 'AFL', as the game is now branded. Commentators need to keep their audiences watching or listening to ensure their ratings remain high, as Dale Holmes, the former AFL executive in charge of NSW football, suggests: 'We take our game seriously and so we want informed commentary, but we also want to entertain as well.'[10]

In addition, the AFL expects their media partners to help sell their product, ensuring their brand of play remains a popular item of consumption in the entertainment industry. Seven Network commentator Tim Watson highlighted this shift:

> There is a fine line here. When you are employed, you are employed by a radio broadcaster or a television network, so your responsibility is to your employer

and therefore, you have to keep people there listening to the radio or you have got to keep them there watching the television… [I]t is an entertainment and as a commentator your responsibility is to provide entertainment.[11]

Rex Hunt, a radio and television broadcaster for more than thirty years, also supports this claim:

> It is an entertainment industry and when I am getting paid a serious amount of money to put the game into the houses of people, I have a responsibility to entertain, because we are a commercial network…and because we are a commercial network and we live and die by the ratings, we have to be entertaining to make sure people listen to us.[12]

This shift in the role of commentators is also evident in the AFL's claim in 2006 that Network Ten commentators Tim Lane and Malcolm Blight had become too negative about the Sydney Swans' game plan and were 'trashing the AFL's brand'.[13] Thus, because of the play–money–media cycle, commentators may apparently no longer speak openly or broadcast the game as they wish.

Performance on the field

Another impact of the play–money–media cycle is reflected in clubs' performance on the field. With the accumulation of economic capital, clubs have the ability to spend significantly higher amounts of money on their football departments (relative to other clubs), which often correlates to better performance on the field. Outlays of economic capital on elite coaches, training equipment, sport sciences and recovery initiatives can and often do, enable players to reach their potential and perform at higher levels of skill than those in opposition clubs which spend less money in these areas. Thus, wealthier clubs often perform better on the field, indicating the existence of a direct link between the amount of economic capital a club can spend on its football department and the overall success of its team. In football clubs, as in society, the rich get richer, despite the AFL's 'equalisation' policy. Scott Hutchins, Geelong member, concurs:

> It definitely helps to be a strong club [financially]. You can employ a greater

number of coaching staff, have more sought after coaching staff and obviously that goes to the back-room people like sport scientists. And particularly now with free agents…the bigger clubs are more likely to command more free agents and bigger names.[14]

Analyses of clubs that have won premierships and those that have not clearly reveal a link between economic capital and performance. Hawthorn, the 2014 premiers, spent $23 million on its team, more than any other Victoria-based team. In 2015, the Fremantle Dockers finished the AFL premiership season on top of the ladder, having spent a total of $24.8 million on their football department the year before. At the other end of the spending list was the Gold Coast Suns, who spent $18.3 million on its football department, less than any other club in the competition. The Suns finished sixteenth (out of eighteen teams) on the AFL ladder.

In recent history, the link between football department spending and on field success has been quite evident. Nine of the past ten premiers were in the top four for football department spending at the time they won their flag. The exception was Geelong in 2007, when the Cats ranked sixth in spending. The last club ranked in the bottom four for football department spending to win a premiership was North Melbourne in 1999 and the last team in the bottom four in expenditures to make the grand final was Melbourne in 2000.[15] According to Michael Westland, an Essendon supporter and member of the AFL, 'You would have to assume and you would annually observe that the teams with more [money], with better facilities…are generally at the top for longer.'[15]

The Fitzroy Football Club is also an example of this link between economic capital and performance on the field. Forced to merge with Brisbane because of its inability to maintain a financially viable team, Fitzroy had won only seven of their last sixty-six AFL matches before the merger. Other traditionally financially insecure clubs have also not won the VFL/AFL premiership in more than fifty years: Melbourne (1964) and St Kilda (1966). The one exception has been North Melbourne. Traditionally one of the poorer clubs in the AFL, North Melbourne won the premiership in 1996 and in 1999.

Pay to play

Another impact of the play–money–media cycle has been the transformation of play into work. As the AFL and its clubs invest considerably in the play element of the game to generate interest in their brands and increase consumption, players have become employees, entertainers at the centre of the AFL's entertainment package. Although the best players have always been paid a small wage to represent their clubs and attract supporters to their games, the amount of money they now receive, along with the rise of celebrity status in the sport field, has escalated with the rise of commercialism and the dominance of economic capital over the last two decades.

In particular, the increasing revenue generated by the AFL from broadcasting rights has resulted in significantly increased wages for players. Total player earnings across the AFL playing list in the 2015 season were $220.54 million. The average salary of an AFL player in 2015 was $302,104. Just under half the players in the AFL (49 per cent) earned between $100,000 and $300,000 for the season, while 33 per cent received between $300,000 and $500,000. In 1990, only 1.5 per cent of players earned between $100,000 and $200,000; and no player earned over $200,000. In 2000, only 5 per cent of players were paid between $300,000 and $500,000. Collectively, the total player payment limit (AFL salary cap) in 2001 was $74,800,000; in 2015, it was $181,284,120, an increase of $106,484,120.[17] Collingwood member Jeremiah Ryan suggests that such wages are reasonable: 'The money's there. The league makes the money and the players are the ones that are providing the product so they are entitled to it… And yes, that's a lot of money, but if you're the very best at what you do, fair enough.'[18] Sydney Swans supporter Cheree Brown concurs: 'Some players are on very high pay packets; however, I think on average it is about right… Football players train hard; they are in the spotlight and dedicate their life to the game. They bring happiness to many fans. They deserve to be paid well.'[19]

Equalisation

For the entertainment package to remain popular among the masses, the game itself must remain entertaining. Therefore, the AFL has assisted the media in ensuring that on-field contests are as close, unpredictable, enthralling and entertaining as possible through the implementation of its equalisation policy. This policy, which has been fundamental to the AFL strategy of ensuring the long-term health of competition since 1985,[20] is designed to help clubs reach their full potential and to ensure they can be active, successful participants in AFL competition. Although this policy appears to be socialistic in its function, purpose and outcomes, it also feeds the play–money–media cycle and emphasises the importance of ensuring play in the AFL is, above all else, entertaining.

According to the AFL website, 'The equalisation policy promotes, but does not guarantee, greater financial stability for individual clubs. It also promotes competitiveness and evenness on the field, allowing for uncertainty of outcomes and the opportunity for surprise results.'[21] Thus, the organisation equally distributes revenues generated by the AFL from broadcasting, corporate sponsorships, finals, preseason competition, corporate hospitality, the *AFL Record* and AFL merchandise sales to its eighteen clubs. In 2015, the AFL distributed $245.15 million.

The equalisation policy is particularly highlighted in the AFL national draft process. Here, the lowest-ranked team from the completed season selects first from the best available talent offered in the first round of the draft; the first-ranked team picks last. Each club is also limited to equal amounts for total player payments (that is, salary caps) to ensure that wealthier clubs cannot purchase the best players by simply offering them more money to play than less wealthy clubs can.[22] Apparently, the equalisation policy is indeed working. Since 1985, all clubs except Gold Coast have made the finals series. Of the other clubs, only Richmond and Greater Western Sydney have not played in an AFL grand final since 1985 and the premiership has been shared by twelve different clubs. Furthermore, throughout any given AFL season, teams near the bottom of the ladder can and do defeat teams near the top of the ladder, meaning 'uncertainty of outcomes and the opportunity for surprise results'[23] do exist.

However, this very objective highlights the influence of the economic and media fields in the sport field, as well as the importance of the equalisation policy as a tool to draw support and generate revenue for the AFL. According to former *AFL Record* editor Peter Di Sisto,

> It [the equalisation policy] has a duel emphasis. It is designed to make all clubs competitive and generally the cycle works, but the bigger issue is that it is a really clever device in that it does work in a business manner was well. It provides a big package that comes together and generates a lot of money. The competition remains competitive so that the interest builds and is covered ad nauseam.[24]

Put simply, the equalisation policy helps the AFL package play as entertainment. By implementing this seemingly socialistic strategy in limiting the power of the rich and distributing wealth to the poor, the AFL ultimately ensures contests on the field remain as close, enthralling and entertaining as possible. Thus, the AFL can maintain the support of every club's fan base, which genuinely believes its team can win or compete against all opposition, regardless of its ladder position. This support translates into television, radio and online audiences, thus increasing AFL broadcast revenues and ensuring steady streams of gate receipts, membership revenues and corporate sponsorships – all of which enhance the AFL brand.

The effects of the play–money–media cycle

The dominance of the economic field and its merger with the sport field, along with the media field, has resulted in an AFL that is only a mirror of what it once was. It simulates pure play; but, in reality, play is now work within a business and a tool of the entertainment industry. Players have become entertainers, paid to play, which puts them at odds with the play element as described by Huizinga:[25] they are no longer entirely free but are employees, committed to their clubs and to the game through binding financial contracts. The teams for which they play are often determined not by the players but by the finances of the clubs involved. Player placement is affected by the total player payment limits imposed by the AFL, resulting in players being traded or delisted because clubs cannot afford to pay them their market value. Such conditions ultimately affect club loyalty, community spirit and passion.

5

The Transformation of the AFL

The landscape of play in the VFL/AFL has changed dramatically over the last 150 years. The influence of the economic and media fields has intensified over the last thirty years, moving the VFL/AFL from a local community-held, grassroots item of folk culture to a multibillion-dollar entertainment industry with a truly national reach. According to Essendon member, Zak Kardachi, the AFL has 'changed the game to a point where if you show someone who had never seen AFL the game ten, fifteen years ago and the game now...it's almost unrecognisable as a game'.

Today, the AFL functions as a business, with its eighteen clubs acting like competing organisations operating within the same industry. Their products are play and their individual brands. Each club sells these products to its supporters (consumers) with the aim of generating enough revenue and profit to survive in the AFL and to gain competitive advantages against the other seventeen clubs. Thus, the influence of the economic and media fields has transformed the AFL in many ways.

The professionalisation of play

In the AFL today, play is a serious matter that bears little resemblance to Huizinga's definition.[1] The increased demands and commitment required of AFL footballers are the result of the professionalisation of the game since the 1990s. Under the umbrella of the VFL, clubs trained twice a week; today, players train nearly every day. Former St Kilda defender and midfielder Austin Jones estimates that most players train with the team for thirty to forty hours per week and then put in an additional fifteen to twenty hours on their own in the form of stretching, recovery, rehabilitation and gym work.² In addition, players must meet media and community work commitments. Together, the training and extra public relations commitments have moved AFL football from the semi-professional, leisure-time pursuit it was in the VFL to a full-time, seven-days-a-week profession.

According to Jones, this shift has fundamentally changed the fun and enjoyment characteristics of the play element: 'The fun in the game has dwindled so much. There's no light moments. It's just a business and that's the sole aim.'³ In the interview, Jones notes that although in his final year of play he received almost a quarter of a million dollars (three times the amount he earned in the first year of his career), he no longer felt the same level of passion and enjoyment when he played, a result of the increased seriousness of play and the demands on players.

James Hird, former Essendon Football Club champion and former coach, shares similar sentiments. Hird, who debuted for the Bombers during the semi-professional era of the game (1992), retired amid the complete professionalisation of the game. He notes the stark difference between the beginning of his career and the ending:

> The thing I miss is, you finish a game of footy, you can't just go out with the whole team and have a few beers. Now if you play at night the recovery finishes at 1.00 am and that prevents that whole team bonding…the footy club is the footy club, but not in the traditional sense any more because of the professionalism you have to keep.⁴

Thus, the merger of the economic and media fields with the sport field has ensured that play is now serious, no longer separate from the ordinary and real and that players no longer enjoy the game to the extent they did before professionalisation.

Not restricted to players, the consequences of the professionalisation have also affected the relationship between the club and its supporters, the people who comprise the club's community and thus the AFL community. Because they need money to survive and flourish as businesses within the AFL and, more broadly, within the entertainment industry, clubs must now act with economic principles and objectives at the forefront of their purpose.

According to Huizinga, a typical sporting club should be a vibrant, central hub of activity where the community meets to enjoy something in common with others. The people who fill the clubroom and the conversations they share should be representative of the broader community and the relationships they share with one another.[5] The club itself should be a meeting point for citizens to connect to their community. However, the transformation of AFL clubs into businesses and their desire to accumulate economic capital to remain viable, vibrant, successful entities within the AFL and entertainment industries have altered their characteristics. The need to generate economic capital has become more important than the community, the grass roots of the club's foundation.

The consequence of this shift is that clubs treat their supporters and communities as consumers of the play element and, therefore, as sources of revenue. Supporters used to be considered custodians of their clubs, whether they contributed financially or not. Now, to be part of the club community, individuals must purchase club memberships. In essence, they must buy a place in their club's community to support the club financially. The club sells the community the message that by purchasing memberships, they are showing 'real' support and displaying their loyalty and passion. In return, they 'own' a piece of the club. In reality, however, members are simply contributing the revenue to the club's need to survive, flourish and ultimately perform at their optimum in the sport field. Thus, the grassroots organisations created and owned by their communities have become businesses selling their products to their consumers.

Memberships comprise a significant portion of club revenues. To meet ever increasing financial needs, clubs have expanded their membership recruitment efforts beyond their traditional grassroots supporter base. In 1997, the Footscray Football Club changed its name to the Western Bulldogs in an attempt to attract supporters from the entire western suburbs area of Melbourne rather than just from the suburb of Footscray.[6] Two years later, the North Melbourne Football Club changed its name to the Kangaroos to garner memberships from throughout the nation rather than just from North Melbourne. (The club changed back to North Melbourne at the end of the 2007 season.[7]) In broadening their supporter base by going outside their home communities, however, clubs have inadvertently disengaged some of their grassroots supporters, who see their clubs placing financial needs and opportunities ahead of their communities and traditional supporters.

The need for revenue has also caused clubs to detach physically from their grassroots foundations. In the last three decades, most of the Victorian clubs have left their traditional home grounds to play at state-of-the-art venues such as the Melbourne Cricket Ground and Etihad Stadium. No longer does Richmond play at Punt Road Oval or Collingwood at Victoria Park or Essendon at Windy Hill. Now they all play their home games at two stadiums located outside their home suburbs.

Many clubs have also abandoned their suburban and community training venues and headquarters for new locations beyond their spiritual supporter base, locations that have little to do with their one-hundred-year history. In 2004, the Collingwood Football Club moved from Victoria Park to the Lexus Centre in Melbourne (now known as the Holden Centre). Soon after, Hawthorn moved its headquarters from Hawthorn to Waverley Park in Mulgrave and St Kilda departed Moorabbin for Seaford. In 2014, Essendon left its spiritual home of Windy Hill for Tullamarine.[8] By moving their headquarters from their spiritual homes and selling home games to interstate locations, clubs have effectively announced the triumph of the entertainment age in which grassroots supporters are consumers, TV audiences and revenue sources. It is an age in which clubs place their needs for economic capital ahead of their traditional and historical roots.

This shift from their grassroots supporters to the entertainment age is also evidenced by the sale of home games to interstate venues and state governments. Several AFL clubs, particularly those more financially vulnerable than their competitors, have engaged in this practice to raise revenue. In doing so, they have effectively denied their supporters and communities the ability to attend games. Hawthorn has contracted with the Tasmanian government to play four games per year at Aurora Stadium in Launceston for an estimated $3.4 million. The club will also receive an extra $1 million from bar sales, gate receipts and sponsorships.[9] North Melbourne has reached a similar agreement with the Tasmanian government to play three games in Hobart for an estimated $1 million per year.[10] Clubs that sold home games to interstate venues in 2016 include Melbourne and the Western Bulldogs.

Most telling in the changes resulting from the professionalisation of the AFL has been the creation of the Gold Coast Suns and the Greater Western Sydney football clubs. These two teams resulted from the AFL's efforts to create new markets and to attract new consumers to the AFL brand, not from grassroots community support. According to Zak Kardachi, money generated from the media was the driving factor in the decision to implement the seventeenth and eighteenth teams in Sydney's west and Queensland's south-east, a way 'to grow the game and overall make the game more profitable'. Elaborating, Kardachi notes that 'if those teams are successful, you then get more people watching the game on TV, you get higher broadcast deals, larger broadcast deals, you get more people buying merchandise, more people going to the games (meaning) revenue overall grows... [Thus,] the AFL placed the importance of money ahead of supporter passion.'

The same lack of consideration for supporters and community is evident in the AFL's decision not to expand into Tasmania. Compared to the Gold Coast and Greater Western Sydney clubs, Tasmania is a relatively smaller market comprised of consumers who are already buying the AFL product even though no Tasmanian team exists. According to Kardachi,

> If the AFL really wanted to love the game...and [to have it] viewed by the people who really want to see it...they'd probably have a team in Tasmania, where there is support – perhaps not commercially as viable support as Greater Western Sydney or the Gold Coast, but definitely a support that is growing for that.[11]

Thus, the need for revenue evidenced by the expansion of AFL teams into new markets rather than into supporter-rich communities highlights the influence of economic capital in the AFL and the transformation of clubs into businesses and supporters into consumers.

Play as entertainment

To ensure the play element remains an attractive revenue-generating item, the AFL must also be concerned with the entertainment value of its product. To that end, the league has often regulated and changed the rules of the game to make it more entertaining in the hope of attracting and keeping more fans. Rule changes include the following:
- deliberate out of bounds,
- deliberate rushed behind,
- time limits for lining up for goals,
- kicking out immediately after the opposition's scoring a behind,
- allowing fewer players on the interchange bench and
- limiting interchange rotations.

Many of these have resulted in a faster game, increasing both the movement within the game and the speed at which the game progresses. All have been introduced to make the game and the play element more aesthetically pleasing and entertaining.[12]

The AFL and the media have also developed off-field extensions of the play element to engage and entertain consumers, including magazine-style football programs and online games. Two such games, Dream Team (operated through the AFL website) and Super Coach (operated through the *Herald Sun* website), allow consumers to choose their own fantasy teams within the restrictions of the AFL-imposed total player payment salary cap. Players are scored and then valued based on how many possessions they accumulate each weekend and by how efficient they are with their disposals.

Both Dream Team and Super Coach reflect the business atmosphere of the AFL. Each player's performance is microanalysed for output and success in terms of efficiency, effectiveness and cost, thus encouraging individualism and microanalysis at the expense of more holistic team analyses. In many ways, as identifying when play begins and ends becomes increasingly difficult, these games blur the distinction between play and ordinary and real life. According to Huizinga, the lack of distinction between these is a characteristic of the corruption of play.[13] Dream Team and Super Coach also illuminate and strengthen the play–money–media cycle. Over 600,000 consumers visit the *Herald Sun* and/or AFL websites each week to play these games (259,927 Australians play Dream Team; 340,441 play Super Coach).[14]

Loyalty

Players in the VFL once followed the unwritten rule that love for the game and for the clubs they represented were more important than opportunities to earn more money elsewhere. Such old-fashioned notions of loyalty and community have all but disappeared, however, as the interconnections among the sport, economic and media fields grow ever stronger. With the AFL and its clubs increasingly utilising players as commodities to 'sell' their products to consumers and strengthen revenue streams, players have become adept at branding themselves and finding ways to capitalise on their commodity status.

The conflict between club loyalty and individual ambition for economic capital is far from new. In 1964, Melbourne Football Club champion Ron Barassi left to captain and coach the Carlton Football Club. This was the first time a champion player of his status had departed his club and community to represent a rival club because of individual desire, ambition and greater financial prosperity. According to John Devaney,

> It was an appointment that sent shock waves reverberating through the entire world of Australian football. To some it seemed as if the very foundation on which the game itself was built had been torn asunder – indeed some maintain that the game has never been the same since.[15]

Thus, as the VFL was transforming into a business and play was evolving into entertainment, the foundations of the game – loyalty, community and tribal spirit – were crumbling, as Devaney notes: 'One of the truisms of Australian football... the old creed of playing for your guernsey – which had been the staple during the Jack Dyer years and so much of the mythology of Australian football around it – was openly challenged.'[16] The mentality of the key stakeholders within the game, the players, was changing, challenging their relationship with their clubs and their communities.

Before the AFL expansion into the northern markets, few big-name players had left their clubs for more money, in part because of the equalisation policy. With each club's expenditure on players capped equally by the AFL, rival clubs found it difficult to lure players from their original clubs by offering them more money. Indeed, the equalisation policy and the salary cap were introduced for this very reason. Even though some high-profile players, such as Chris Judd, left their original clubs for more money, most players remained loyal to the clubs that first drafted them. That began to change with the creation of the Gold Coast Suns and Greater Western Sydney.

The expansion, along with the intense desire within the AFL to appeal to consumers in these new markets, compromised the equalisation policy and threatened the notion of loyalty. The AFL excluded the Gold Coast Suns and the Greater Western Sydney Giants from their strict salary cap, giving them more money ($750,000 and $1 million, respectively) than their sixteen counterparts to attract high-profile players to their clubs to build their playing lists.[17] More money meant greater power and ability to recruit players through financial incentives. This led some of the biggest names in Australian football – indeed, in the Australian sporting landscape – to abandon their home clubs and communities to earn significantly more money.

Defections from home clubs to join AFL playing lists have not been confined to the AFL. In 2009, a National Rugby League (NRL) player, Karmichael Hunt, shocked the Australian sporting industry by leaving the NRL to play Australian football for the Gold Coast Suns. Hunt reportedly signed a three-year contract for $3 million, effectively making him one of the most highly paid players in the AFL.[18] This caused unprecedented furore among the AFL clubs and players, because a man who had never previously played the game of Australian football at the highest level and was far from the best player in sport had become one of the highest paid players in the AFL competition.[19] In their desire to sell their brands, the AFL and the Gold Coast Suns invested in Hunt to garner advertising and public relations to promote the new club. Hunt was not just a player; he was a tool to market and sell the AFL and Suns brands and to attract new supporters not only to the game but also to their television sets to watch Hunt and his teammates play. Thus, Hunt's defection is a shining example of the commodification of the game: economic capital lured Hunt away from rugby league, the game he knew and had played with spontaneous instinct from his childhood, to a game he had played sparingly as a teenager and never in a professional setting.

A little over a year later, the lure of economic capital trumped the notion of loyalty once again. Gary Ablett, arguably the best player in the AFL, defected from his original club, the Geelong Cats, to the Gold Coast Suns for a reported $9 million over five years.[20] What made this even more remarkable was Ablett's connection to the Geelong Football Club and the Geelong community. Ablett grew up barracking for the Geelong Cats. His father, Gary Ablett senior (considered one of the greatest VFL/AFL players of all time) had played 242 games for the club. Because of his father's thirteen-year career with the Cats, Geelong selected seventeen-year-old Ablett junior under the AFL's father-son rule. Ablett junior played 192 games for Geelong, won two Best and Fairest awards for the club and a Brownlow Medal and played in two Geelong premiership teams. However, the enticement of $9 million over five years was enough for Ablett to defect.

Even though the prospect of pioneering the development of a new club and being the first Gold Coast captain undoubtedly influenced him, it's difficult to imagine that Ablett would have departed had Geelong offered him the same or similar money. Of course, Geelong could not do so because of the significant amounts of economic capital the AFL infused into Gold Coast and Greater Western Sydney to sign high-profile celebrity players.[21]

AFL supporters vary in their opinions about Ablett's defection. Stuart Osbourne notes, 'I don't begrudge him…it was hard, like he'd been offered money that sets him up for life, that Geelong could never match… I don't begrudge him the decision at all.' Tom Gallimore concurs: 'As I said before about player management and what not…there's only a certain amount of time you're going to be able to make money.'[22] However, Michael Westland holds the opposite view: 'I consider myself a loyal person – quite a fierce loyal person [and] to give up [a] big part of you for money when you probably don't need it when living on 500 grand or a million and half [a year]… I think I wouldn't have made the same decision.' As far as players in general are concerned, Cheree Brown views leaving for better money as being 'similar to a promotion'; but for Effie Caloutas, player loyalty is important. In her view, players who leave their teams for more money are being disrespectful of the clubs that 'had an impact on their career[s]'.[23]

In 2010, the AFL enticed another NRL player, Israel Folau, to defect from the NRL to the Greater Western Sydney Giants for a reported $6 million over four years, effectively making him the highest paid Australian footballer in the country.[24] The Giants recruited Folau, a well-known entity in Sydney who grew up in Western Sydney, to help sell the Giants team and brand to the Greater Western Sydney market. Despite the fact that he had never played Australian football at any level of competition in his life, the media strategy largely worked. The announcement of Folau's defection generated more than 6,311 newspaper, TV and radio media stories, for an estimated $12.3 million-worth of media coverage for the AFL and the Greater Western Sydney Giants. Newspapers featured the announcement on their front and back pages on forty-six occasions in the first two days of Folau's signing. The vast majority of that coverage was within New South Wales and Queensland, the AFL's target growth markets.[25]

Folau's defection did not receive universal support across the NRL and AFL landscapes, however. Many within the AFL bemoaned the move and were hostile towards the idea that the game's highest paid athlete was a twenty-two-year-old man who had never played the game at any level of competition in his life. They also believed that Folau lacked a certain sense or feel for the game that his opponents and teammates enjoyed because they had played the game their whole lives. Therefore, Folau did not deserve more money than his teammates or opponents who could perform better during games.[26] In fact, Folau failed as a player, while Hunt was at best a modest success, and both later left the game to pursue a career in rugby union.

The Folau and Hunt recruitments say much about the influence of money and media in the sport field. For money, both defected from games they loved, to play a game they had never played before, at least not at elite levels of competition. Both were used as publicity tools to promote play in the AFL above all other items of entertainment that compete for the hearts and minds of Australian consumers in the NSW and Queensland markets. As Essendon supporter Jason Lee observes, 'It was a branding exercise, purely. You're getting two central figures in another code [and] converting them over. They [the AFL] wanted to hit the target audience of the young kids following NRL.'[27]

Other supporters and club members shared similar sentiments. Collingwood member Jeremiah Ryan notes that 'the AFL didn't go out and pay for players. They went out and bought profiles. They went out and identified players that were already popular with sport viewers in these areas where the AFL was trying to expand… They bought their profile for marketing.' Scott Hutchins, a member of the Geelong Football Club, sees Hunt and Folau as 'marketing tools' that the AFL 'was using… to establish fans in rugby states'. According to Phil Wilde, recruiting Hunt and Folau was 'purely marketing…getting names that New South Wales, Sydney-siders in particular, would look at and stand up and take notice'.[28] Josh Forte, Hawthorn Football Club member and supporter, agrees that the acquisitions were market-driven but believes that 'it was a terrific decision'. Although having these two NRL stars play for the AFL 'may not have made an NRL fan become an AFL fan', Forte notes that 'it certainly made them think about the game and it would've flooded the media in those northern states'.[29] Essendon supporter Michael Westland also feels the AFL acted appropriately in recruiting these players: 'If you were trying to make a foothold in a new market…you've got to find some way of relating to the people in the market. But more than that, you have to make waves… So I think the AFL made absolutely the right decision.'

The recruitments of Hunt and Ablett to the Suns and of Folau, Callan Ward (from the Western Bulldogs) and Tom Scully (from Melbourne) to the Giants[30] highlight just how much play has changed since the founding of the game in 1858, changes resulting from the influence of the economic and media fields and the play–money–media cycle. However, the impacts of the merging of these three fields have not been confined to player recruitment. Indeed, the introduction of free agency at the end of the 2012 AFL season has amplified the influence of economic capital and its antagonistic relationship with loyalty and community.

Free agency

Beginning with the 2013 season, AFL clubs can offer players who have played on rival teams for more than eight seasons financial contracts for sums greater than those their current teams are paying. The home clubs may match offers made to any of their ten highest paid players but not to any of the other players on their teams. Players then have the right to accept the rival clubs' offers or not. Thus, clubs with the most money available under their total player payment salary cap can offer rival players significant pay increases to defect from their original clubs. More important, however, is that players will increasingly determine who they will play for based on how much money they can earn at any given club, as Lance 'Buddy' Franklin's defection from Hawthorn to the Sydney Swans at the end of the 2013 AFL season highlights.

Taking advantage of free agency, at the age of twenty-six Franklin signed a contract worth $10 million over nine years to play for the Sydney Swans, an offer his home club, Hawthorn, simply could not match. He declared his intent to leave Hawthorn for Sydney just two days after Hawthorn had triumphed in the grand final to win the 2013 AFL premiership, placing money ahead of the bonds and connections he had formed with his Hawthorn teammates and community. Thus, economic capital has become the most influential bargaining tool and determining factor of a player's participation in the sport field.

Although clubs can, and most likely will, continue to depend upon loyalty and creeds of playing for the jumper, the influence of economic capital is difficult to ignore. Gary Ablett, Karmichael Hunt, Israel Folau and others have already proved that the enticement of more money is difficult to ignore.[31] The advent of free agency not only places economic capital at the forefront of the sport field but also potentially diminishes loyalty and the significance of community as reasons for representing AFL clubs. Even though players still enjoy some sense of community and friendship among the players and supporters of the clubs they represent, no player in the AFL plays for free; and, considering they are the performers of the show, nobody expects them to do so. Thus, as retired Essendon, Brisbane and Collingwood defender Mal Michael states, 'The problem is we sign contracts and when they expire, that's it – there is no loyalty.'[32] This was further illustrated towards the end of the 2016 season when Brent Harvey, the holder of the record for the number of games played (432), was told by his club, North Melbourne, that they would not renew his contract once it expired at season's end. The veteran player had played twenty-one seasons for the Kangaroos and was adored by the North Melbourne faithful. However, in the clinical world of AFL business, sentiment and loyalty could not win Harvey an extension of his contract.

The coaches

Because the play element is at the heart of the images and brands of the AFL and its clubs, being successful on the field is vitally important to the vibrancy of business operations. Therefore, clubs spend significant time, effort and resources to ensure successful on-field performance, including the development of well-equipped football departments and significant increases in the number of people responsible for managing the athletes and the play element.

As the professionalisation of the game grows, so does the influence of coaches on the way the game is played. Fans are keenly aware of the differences in coaches since the professionalisation of the sport. According to Jason Lee, coaches were originally responsible for motivating players, delivering 'fire and brimstone sort of stuff'. Now, however, 'it's very strategic. It's tactical. There's sport science involved…they analyse the opposition very closely', noting the various coaches' responsibilities for gathering statistical information during each game: tactical information that comes through different line coaches…a forward coach, a back coach, a mid coach, a ruck coach, a specialist coach for kicking…a coach for marking… Twenty years ago, you had one coach and it was his message and that was the way it was.' Cheree Brown also acknowledges that 'the approach' coaches now use 'is much more methodical'. Jeremiah Ryan suggests that teams today have more coaches than they used to have: 'developing coaches and tactical analysts and guys that don't even see their own club play. All they do is…research on the opposition… [Y]ou can't for a minute think that footy hasn't changed with regards to tactics and the development and innovation of how they process information.' Kate Withers concurs, noting that 'the role has become so specific and niche' that she 'doubt[ed] any club could compete with a sole head coach'.

Supporters have also noted the increasing importance of coaches and the decreasing role of players in managing the play element. Effie Caloutas states that although 'players are responsible for meeting the coaches' needs and executing the game plan required…coaches have an even bigger influence because they have to create a suitable game plan'. According to Michael Westland, 'A coach has influence over how the game's played and the mindset of the players and the performance of players and I think that would far outweigh the (influence of) the best player.' For Stuart Osbourne, regardless of all the 'talk about recruiting and a lot of other factors…there has to be a vision that comes from the coach or the football manager'. Therefore, coaches have the biggest influence because 'the trend in football and the way the game has changed over the last ten years has been driven by coaches trying to get the best competitive advantage on the field'. Jason Lee concurs: 'The coaches…are able to put their blueprint down for how the side wants to play. The player's obviously responsible for carrying that out, but the coach provides the mandate and the plan.' In terms of his own club, Hawthorn, Joshua Forte feels that the head coach is 'the visionary for our club'. The coach has been working with a 'core group of players since they were young men…growing up and evolving with him… I have no doubt that before the game, the coach's philosophies are being drummed into them and then, more often that not, adhered to on the ground.'

However, not all of the fans I interviewed agree. Jeremiah Ryan feels that 'the players have the greater influence because they're the ones who kick the scores'. He suggests that 'the AFL's really been wrestling with the coaches to try and get it [the play product] to what the AFL wants it to look like. But the coaches don't care about how the footy looks, the coaches care about winning games… And that's why the AFL's been sort of changing certain rules…[which] pushes against the way coaches have been trying to take the game.' Geelong member Scott Hutchins argues for the players: 'You've got about ten or twelve guys who have been at the club for a long time and have played some successful football and they've played mostly in the same manner…[and] they're still our most influential players, so they sort of dictate in a sense how they play.' Ultimately, the players are more important because, as Cheree Brown notes, regardless of how good any coach may be, 'if he does not have the depth of talent in his team to execute it [the game plan], they will still lose'.

Nevertheless, anecdotal evidence shows that members of each team's football department, especially the coaches, are now shaping the play element. Play in the AFL is no longer only an exuberant, energetic contest between two teams striving towards a shared and common goal. It is an important function of business. Coaches analyse the play just as any manager analyses key functions in any business, with winning being the key performance indicator for the club's business objectives. No longer do the outcomes of matches have consequences only for those who play, coach or support the team; they now have consequences for the other business objectives of the club. Memberships, merchandise sales, crowd attendance and television ratings are all dependent on the on-field success of the team.

Thus, coaches and players now plan meticulously for each AFL match. They monitor and analyse the way team members play, both individually and collectively, to ensure optimum performance and to improve their chances of winning. Players are expected to carry out the instructions of coaches and play certain roles within the team and teams are expected to play within the confines of the coaches' overarching tactics and structures. As Michael Westland points out in referring to 'player's interviews about structure', the players are quite cognisant of these changes to the play element:

> It's no longer about me manning Joe Bloggs for 120 minutes. It's about me marking, playing as a defender and me and my other five defenders marking a zone, an area of about 50 [metres] that the ball no longer penetrates... We might have to mark our man for any length of time but as long as we, as five or six do our jobs together, we will win more games than we lose. And then...that six becomes eight becomes twelve becomes eighteen on a field – all marking areas and zones rather than beating their individual opponents.

Supporters are also aware of the increased analysis of games and the overall increase in the use of strategy to win. As Sydney supporter Phil Wild notes, 'Ten years ago, you might have said, "Just kick it to Jonathon Brown, he'll take care of it." Now, everyone [is] playing a similar style of game, with a few modifications, based on maybe a few star players.'[33]

The consequences

Huizinga believes fun and enjoyment are the bases for play. Play should be free and spontaneous, 'a discharge of superabundant energy to seek the satisfaction of some imitative instinct'.[34] If players no longer have fun or are not enjoying themselves, they are no longer playing. Instead, they are working. The increasing influence of coaches and the use of microanalysis, tactics and strategies have affected the flair, freedom, spontaneity, creativity and enjoyment of players, which fans clearly recognise. According to Jeremiah Ryan, 'A well drilled team, it plays the way the coach wants them to play… [The players] have almost no creative control.' Alanna Ford concurs: 'Much of the personality has gone out of the game.' She specifically referenced Dusty (Dustin) Martin, 'an electrifying performer but with an edge, you never know if he is going to step out of line – but the minute somebody does, good old-fashioned "theatrics" are shot down, penalised and over-analysed by the media… The days of iconic match ups between two formidable opponents have gone.' Josh Forte comments that players in the past had 'so much flair, so much personality on the field… so much creativity for their team and maybe not the most athletically gifted, which is brilliant football to watch. Whereas now you find more brilliant teams than brilliant players.'

For Tom Gallimore, however, the issue is not clear-cut:

> I think it depends on who you are as a player, how much trust the coach has in you as a player. I think you need to be able to manage and temper your flair and your creativity. But I think good players can do that. The good players can step up when they need to and show individual brilliance and flair, but they can equally know when to offload to a player that's 20 metres out in front of them, that guarantees you get a goal.

Stuart Osbourne offers a different perspective:

> I think all players in all teams play a role as part of the system of play that their coach wants them to play. I don't think, however, there are any players that fully go out there and play with freedom and flair…every player goes out there to play the role, but because it's so systematic…players who do have that freedom and flair to play actually have more ability to shine.

For Michael Westland, flair and freedom versus restricted control is more a matter of decision making:

> I don't think you'll ever take the individual flair and spontaneity and decision making away from an individual. More and more they're playing more to a game plan, a structure…but when a player gets the ball…you can't remove

that decision making prowess from an individual, but more and more when the ball's not with them or the ball's moved away from their area, they no longer think [for themselves]...[they now think] where does the coach want me to be and that's where they go.

On the other side, Scott Hutchins argues that the changes have not affected player freedom, despite the increasing 'talk about the structures and the systems that a team wants to play'. He believes as many 'players with individual flair' exist in the 'competition now as there's ever been... and they still get a chance to show their flair...a player's individual flair and brilliance is always going to overshine the coaches' team structures and systems'.

Nevertheless, the majority of the supporters I interviewed perceive that coaches have altered the play element in the AFL. These fans also believe the transformation of play is not restricted to the AFL but is also evident within local and grassroots football. Both Phil Wild and Josh Forte, as noted earlier in this chapter, discussed the changes wrought by the introduction of more strategy and role definition, the increased instructions from coaches and the issue of player pay on local teams.

The merger of the sport field with the economic and media fields has ensured that AFL football now mirrors the bureaucratic business model of contemporary Western society in that all the key stakeholders (players, coaches, administrators and board members) now make decisions based on economic rationalism objectives. The merger has also ensured that player profiles and income potential are not restricted to the sport field. Players receive exposure through all forms of media more than ever before because of the saturated coverage of the AFL and its clubs. Media personnel interview players before, during and after televised games and profile them in print and on TV and radio programs. Players appear on entertainment programs such as *The Footy Show* and *Game Day* and draw mass followers and fans through their own social media channels, such as Twitter and Facebook.

With the transformation of play to display has come the celebrity status of players, who have recognition and power both inside and outside the sport field. As such, they have become tools utilised not only by the AFL and its clubs but also by companies external to the AFL to market, advertise and sell products and services. These companies believe that endorsements by popular sport celebrities will result in increased sales and revenue. Such endorsements have also allowed players to garner even greater amounts of money outside the field of play than their contracted salaries.

Thus, as Huizinga feared, playing for pay has damaged the essential play characteristics of fun and spontaneity.[35] Indeed, the increased influence of economic capital in the AFL has coincided with a decrease in the fun and enjoyment players experience when actively participating in play in the AFL. As Austin Jones states, 'It's [the game] just a business and that's the sole aim.'[36]

The transformation of the AFL into a business and a form of entertainment is also linked fundamentally with the performance of each AFL team on the field. Economic capital has inextricably intertwined on-field success (winning) with off-field success (financial growth). Likewise, if an AFL club is financially prosperous, its team is more likely to be successful on the field, which has direct consequences for the play element, the integrity of the game and the strength of the AFL community.

6

The Manipulation and Corruption of Play

Winning needs no explanation; losing has no alibi. – Greg Baum

Winning has been an essential part of Australian football since its inception. Both the players and the teams have always taken great pride in playing to their optimum capability and beating their opponents. Likewise, the people who watch and barrack for their clubs admire the most skilful, talented and fairest teams and individuals. The goal is winning the premiership; and players, supporters and clubs all work together in this shared passion to achieve this common goal. Scores determine the winners and losers of individual games. Based on these data, teams are placed on a ladder in the order of their performance (wins, losses and draws) throughout the season to determine the best teams. The best teams enter a final series of contests to determine the grand final participants and ultimate winner, which is declared the premiership team.[1]

Individual players also receive recognition for being the best. All the AFL teams bestow the Best and Fairest Award to the player who is judged the fairest and best player and who has contributed the most toward helping the team win. Many of the AFL's oldest clubs have a long and proud history of recognising their most talented, skilful and courageous players, presenting them with a range of awards and rewards at the end of the season. Often these honours are named after former champion players. Indeed, one of the AFL's most prestigious awards is the Brownlow Medal, awarded to the player judged by the umpires as the AFL's fairest and best.[2] The Brownlow Medal is widely considered the highest individual honour an AFL player can receive. In addition to the Brownlow Medal and the Best and Fairest Awards are other individual awards, including Most Valuable Player (awarded by the Players' Association), the Coaches Award (awarded by the clubs' eighteen head coaches) and selection to the all-Australian team (the best twenty-two players of the season). Team success, however, has always been considered the players' primary objective. Individual awards are merely recognition of individuals' contributions to the success of their respective teams.

Although wanting and trying to win and striving to be the best are far from new, the influence of other fields on the AFL has affected who recognises these players and teams and the kinds of awards and rewards they receive. Before the influence of the economic and media fields, players and teams who were successful received recognition, respect, even adoration, mostly from key participants within the sport field. They gained little capital, if any, in other fields. Winning the title of premiership team or the Brownlow Medal might enhance a player's reputation within the AFL (that is, enhanced social capital), but such awards did not significantly increase the player's power and reputation outside the AFL. Achieving success on the field with their teammates and celebrating with those who had worked hard to achieve a common goal was largely considered reward enough. This is no longer the case.

As the economic field increasingly influences the sport field, the emphasis on winning, and the subsequent by-product of being recognised as the best, is increasingly linked to economic capital, especially money. Team performance on the field affects the club's brand, which, in turn, affects the club's ability to generate revenue. Winning teams attract more supporters, members and spectators, which increase gate revenues. More people attending and watching games means more people likely to purchase club merchandise, again increasing revenues. Winning also attracts more corporate sponsors and their dollars. The more games played during prime time television and its bigger audiences, the more revenue generated. The more revenue, the more money available to attract and develop the best players and coaches and to purchase the best, and often most expensive, training equipment and player development programs – all to ensure the successful on-field performance of the team and the attractiveness of the club brand to other prospective sources of revenue.

The off-field consequences of poor on-field performance are a less attractive brand and diminished capacity to earn money. As Tom Gallimore, Brisbane Lions supporter, observes,

> I think with any sporting code, if they are not winning, it makes it tough. It flows down from the players through the coaches, through the sponsors, through the fans…sponsors want the club that they're associated with to be winning. They want to be seen in a positive light…it gets fans through the gate and it gets fans engaged in their brand.

In talking about the consequences of the poor on-field performance his Brisbane Lions were experiencing, he notes that 'they lost their two major sponsors…which is huge… [M]anagement and the club boards and organisations hope…their team wins as much as possible because it relieves pressure on partnerships, sponsors, but it also keeps fans engaged, excited, coming through the gates, all turning up and purchasing merchandise or watching it [the game] online and paying that way.'

Likewise, players who receive recognition through any of the individual awards mentioned previously can rightly expect sponsors to approach them. Companies external to the AFL utilise players as commodities, approaching them to serve as ambassadors or to give endorsements for their brands and products. The top players can earn thousands of dollars in addition to their club earnings by accepting these sponsorships.

Although revenue generation has existed since the creation of the VFL, never has it been more blatant than today. Once defined as achieving a shared goal with the club's community, team success is now a vehicle to drive revenue. Thus, AFL clubs tend to operate less as communities and more as businesses. More important, though, is the accompanying pressure from the economic field to be successful, which has resulted in some clubs manipulating the play element to win.

Manipulating play can occur in many ways, some illegal or unethical, others legal but in violation of the spirit of the game:

(a) tanking, the deliberate losing of games to gain an advantage in the drafting process;
(b) both appropriate and inappropriate application of sport science to improve performance; and
(c) match fixing.

Here we examine examples of each of these issues that have been investigated by the AFL since the 2009 season.

Tanking

During the 2012 football season, the AFL's Integrity Unit began an investigation into allegations that the Melbourne Football Club had tanked during the 2009 AFL premiership season to win a priority selection in the national draft. Under the AFL's equalisation policy at the time, teams that finished the twenty-two game season with no more than four wins automatically received a 'priority pick', meaning they had two picks at the beginning of the draft instead of one. This provision effectively gave such teams two chances to secure the best young talent in the country.[3]

Tanking refers to losing intentionally or failing to compete.[4] In many ways the antithesis of Huizinga's notion of play,[5] tanking is achieved by players, coaches or management manipulating and corrupting play to control the play element to achieve a desired result. Tanking stands in direct opposition to the original purpose of sporting clubs and the building of community.

Accusations of tanking on the part of Melbourne came from supporters, commentators and observers. Although few doubted that the players who took the field tried their best to win every game in which they played, many argued that the coaches and administrators had selected teams that could not win and had fielded players in positions that ensured the team could not perform at its best, damaging their chances to win. In effect, it was argued that Melbourne's coaches and administrators had tried to manipulate the play element to lose by ensuring their team could not perform optimally.

In addition, many believed Melbourne thought the club could neither be successful nor climb the AFL ladder unless it added young talent to its playing list – and the club wanted the best young talent available. By losing in 2009, Melbourne believed it could draft the key players necessary to ensure its future. Thus, the club was willing to suffer short-term pain for long-term gain.

The actual investigation into the Melbourne Football Club was triggered by Brock McLean, a Melbourne player during the 2009 season, who stated on Fox Footy's *On the Couch* program that blind Freddy could see that Melbourne had deliberately not tried to win some games in the 2009 season.[6] The investigators conducted fifty-eight interviews, talking with both current and former players, coaches, administrators and club officials. The AFL also undertook forensic analysis of the Melbourne Football Club's computers, files and email system. The investigation revealed the following:[7]

- Neither the Melbourne Football Club board nor the club's executive management had issued any directive that the team should deliberately lose matches throughout the 2009 premiership season.
- Neither the club nor its coaches or team had set out deliberately to lose any matches.
- Chris Connolly, the General Manager of Football Operations for the Melbourne Football Club, had made comments in a football department meeting concerning pregame planning which were prejudicial to the interests of the AFL. He was alleged to have warned an estimated fifteen Melbourne officials against the perils of winning more than four games for the season.
- Dean Bailey, the Melbourne Football Club 2009 senior coach, acted upon Connolly's comments, resulting in behaviour prejudicial to the interests of the AFL.

Based on the findings, which were released on 19 February 2013, Melbourne was found not guilty of tanking during the 2009 AFL season but did receive the following sanctions:[8]

- Chris Connolly was suspended until 1 February 2014, from occupying any office or performing any function, including attending matches or training sessions, for or on behalf of any club. The suspension commenced on Monday, 25 February 2013.

- Dean Bailey was suspended from coaching for the first sixteen rounds of the 2013 premiership season. During this time, he was not permitted to have any match-day role working with players. He could, however, remain an employee of the Adelaide Football Club if the club desired.
- The Melbourne Football Club accepted ultimate responsibility for the conduct of its key personnel and agreed to pay a fine of $500,000.

The AFL also stated that although the draft rules allow for the distribution of elite talent among the AFL clubs to ensure their long-term future, the rules absolutely do not allow teams to manipulate the draft or total player payment provisions for their own ends. To make it harder to qualify for priority selection for poor performance, the league altered these rules at the start of the 2012 season. Under the current AFL rules, enacted from the 2012 season onwards, a club can receive a priority draft pick at the discretion of the AFL Commission.

Although few, if any, ever suggested that the Melbourne players who took the field each weekend did not try their best to win each match, the AFL's findings indicate that the play element was managed, controlled, manipulated and corrupted to ensure Melbourne did not win more than four games for the season. In effect, the players were positioned to ensure that, more often than not, they could not reach their full potential and, thus, were not given the best chance of winning. Thus, the influence of the economic field and the structure of the modern football club allowed Melbourne Football Club officials to manipulate the play element to lose.

Not only does such behaviour stand in direct opposition to Huizinga's definition of pure play, but it weakens the club community. Community is built upon the notion of citizens coming together to enjoy something in common with each other while striving towards a shared common outcome or goal. If the common goal the majority of club members are working towards is corrupted by coaches or administrators conspiring to lose games, then surely the community is also corrupted. No longer is the whole community working for the same outcome. Supporters expect players and coaches to prepare and to play to the best of their abilities and support them in achieving success.

Several of the fans I interviewed were definitely opposed to their clubs tanking, even if refraining from doing so cost them priority draft selections. For Scott Hutchins, entertaining the idea of tanking is tantamount to 'planting the seed in their [players'] mind[s] that winning is not the ultimate game'. He considers this 'detrimental in the long run' because the notion can become 'ingrained in people [and] they can lose their appetite for the contest'. To illustrate his point, he cites the Melbourne case. Jason Lee objects on similar grounds:

> You always want to see your team with a desire to achieve and the minute that stops I think you can destroy the soul of a club and I think you've seen that with what's happened at Melbourne... I see it as a cancer... [T]he moment you let that into a club or an organisation...that's a very dangerous psyche to bring into a club and it's very hard to get it out.

Stuart Osbourne is opposed to the idea because 'it's fundamental to competitive sport that both teams go out with the intent to try to win'. He also notes the consequences of tanking to the culture of the club:

> If you create a culture where anything but winning is acceptable or anything but giving it your most, then you create a losing culture and then it becomes hard to win.

Two of the interviewees hold broader views. Tom Gallimore considers tanking to be 'unAustralian'. He also focuses on a different financial aspect of the game, stating that even though players 'get paid a lot of money...some teams aren't going to have a great year'. In such situations, however, players should still be 'giving it [their] all'. Zak Kardachi is the most vehement of the interviewees who oppose tanking, considering it 'the same as stealing':

> You always know that you effectively cheated. You broke the rules, you subverted the rules, you took advance of the rules and you did something that is not in the spirit of the game or the spirit of the club in order to possibly secure a future.

Interestingly, although the women I interviewed were against the idea of tanking, their reasons had more to do with how the supporters might view clubs that did so. Pride in a 'team that plays with integrity and honesty and loses' is more important to Kate Withers than a team that 'may or may not improve because they have tanked for draft picks'. Cheree Brown 'enjoy[s] going to the footy and watching them perform to the best of their ability', noting she 'would be so disappointed if they did not give 100% and tried to lose'. For Effie Caloutas, tanking results in a more practical problem for clubs: 'Tanking to finish down the bottom of the ladder would only lose supporters, as supporters want to see their team succeed on the field.' Although she acknowledges that getting first draft picks is not 'worth the feeling of humiliation and deflations as you slide down the ladder' that comes with tanking, Alanna Ford notes that ultimately some clubs are simply 'better at recruiting than others'.

Yet not all football fans are against the idea of their teams tanking to receive priority draft selections at the AFL national draft. Collingwood supporter Jeremiah Ryan states, 'I'm hoping that we lose. I'm hoping that we drop our half dozen best players and play an extra six kids and give them exposure to senior football.' Josh Forte and Michael Westland concur. Forte even believes that 'it would be remiss of a club not to tank… you would be crazy not to influence games to lose'. Westland is a bit more ambivalent. Although he 'probably would' support his team tanking, he also 'would want the players to go out and give their all'.

Although Melbourne was found not to have tanked during the 2009 season, the issue and resulting investigation highlight the influence of the economic field in reshaping the structure of football clubs to mirror businesses. As such, various levels of management can influence the outcomes of matches through micromanaging, a direct reflection of the economic field in sport. Although Melbourne's management did not influence the actual play element during the football games and, therefore, did not harm the integrity of the play element, the AFL investigation found they did affect the team's potential to play at its best, to reach their potential and to win. Thus, management damaged the very principle on which AFL football teams and their resulting communities were created. Were the AFL an autonomous organisation rather than a business, players and coaches working together to perform optimally to win would determine the outcomes of games.

Further revealing the influence of the economic field and subsequent commercialisation of the AFL is the very reason some within the Melbourne Football Club might have been willing to lose consistently during the 2009 season: being successful in the future to improve their brand. Doing so would provide significantly more potential to earn money so that the club could remain successful both on and off the field. Those who advocated losing did so as a means of eventually improving the club brand through accumulating players good enough to win more often than not. The club could then climb the AFL ladder and attract more supporters, members and sponsors, continuing the play–money–media cycle.

The support of some AFL fans for this type of manipulation also illuminates the overarching business characteristic of the AFL: making short-term compromises in the interest of long-term success that can be sustained on and off the field. Thus, tanking is one possible result of the influence of money and the commercial benefits that winning provides. This influence has led to a 'whatever it takes' and 'win at all costs' mentality within the AFL, a mentality that has also caused clubs to draw on other notable fields to gain advantages over their opponents. One such field is the field of sport science.

Sport science

On 6 February 2013, the Essendon Football Club asked the AFL and the Australian Sport Anti-Doping Agency (ASADA) to investigate the club amid uncertainty concerning the legality of substances administered to its players during the 2012 pre-season. At the centre of ASADA's investigation was the club's use of peptides and the specific way in which the supplements were administered.[9] Peptides are compounds composed of amino acid molecules, many of which are legal for elite athletes to take. Some peptides, however, promote muscle growth and have properties similar to those found in human growth hormone (HGH). According to WebMD.com, HGH is produced by the pituitary gland and spurs growth in children and adolescents. It also helps to regulate body composition, body fluids, muscle and bone growth, sugar and fat metabolism and possibly heart function.[10] As such, the World Anti-Doping Authority (WADA) prohibits the use of HGH both in and out of competition and lists it on the WADA list of prohibited substances and methods.[11]

Players found to have used or to have attempted to use banned substances are effectively found guilty of cheating. In using substances which enable the body to perform above its natural capability and potential, athletes eliminate the essence of fair play because they have an unfair and unnatural advantage. Thus, players caught with any prohibited substances in their systems receive severe penalties, as illustrated in the cases of lower level rugby union players Trent Anderson and Mitchell Spackman. Both received two-year suspensions for their involvement with growth hormone peptide 6 (GHRP-6). Anderson's sanction was for possession and attempted use; Spackman's was for attempted use.[12]

Competitors within the sport field who gain unfair advantages through the act of cheating threaten the very foundation on which sport is built and defined. In particular, they corrupt the play element by using science to manipulate it to the point that the contest is no longer fair. The consequences of this extend beyond individual or team sanctions. As mentioned previously, sport clubs and communities are built upon a shared and common passion (play) which is utilised by its members to work together to achieve a shared, common objective (winning). For sporting clubs to stimulate communities, those involved not only must have a shared passion for play but also must believe that the shared objective is achievable. More important, they must believe that they can achieve their goal within the rules and that their competitors are also working together and acting within the rules. This ensures the integrity of the sport field. Thus, individuals or clubs who cheat corrupt not only the play element but also its ability to stimulate community.

The narrative of the AFL media covering the Essendon supplements story focused heavily on the role of the senior coach, James Hird. As a former champion player and premiership captain of the club, he was seen as 'the saviour' by many Essendon supporters when he returned to the club as senior coach in 2011. Upon his return, he implemented a 'whatever it takes' approach to return the club to the top of the AFL ladder after years of mediocrity. With an ambition to achieve instant success, Hird endorsed the appointment of Stephen Dank, a so-called sports scientist, who implemented and led the club's supplements program from late 2011 until September 2012.[13]

In August 2013, ASADA submitted an interim report of its investigation of the Essendon Football Club to the AFL, which had not found the club guilty of either substance abuse or cheating. The AFL utilised the interim report to charge four Essendon officials of bringing the game into disrepute and subsequently suspended senior coach James Hird from working at Essendon or any other AFL club for twelve months. Although Hird returned to coach the Essendon Football club for the 2015 season, he resigned on 17 August 2015.

Five months earlier, on 31 March 2015, an independent AFL Anti-Doping Tribunal found thirty-four current and former Essendon players not guilty of using a banned supplement during the 2012 football season. However, on 11 May, WADA announced it would appeal the not guilty decision to the Court of Arbitration for Sport. The hearing was heard over five days from 16 to 20 November 2015. On 12 January 2016, the Court of Arbitration for Sport found thirty-four past and present players guilty of being injected with banned peptide Thymosin Beta 4. They were subsequently banned from participating in the 2106 AFL season.[14] On 10 February, an appeal against the findings was lodged by the players to the Federal Supreme Court of Switzerland.[15] However, the appeal failed.

Because of the importance of winning to both on- and off-field stability and prosperity sport clubs and athletes are increasingly pushing the boundaries of fairness and legality to gain advantages over their opponents. Thus, the economic field has become a key facilitator in the increasing role of sport science in the AFL. Where once players relied only on hard work and ability to win football games, they now also rely on sport scientists to provide supplements and dietary advice to ensure sustained optimum performance. Although perfectly legal (unless a breach of ASADA regulations), the utilisation of sport science also illuminates the increased management of play from various levels of administration within AFL clubs.

Two days after Essendon asked the AFL and ASADA to assist them in reviewing their 2012 supplements program, the Australian Crime Commission (ACC) released results from a twelve-month investigation which found strong evidence of the use of banned substances among athletes in multiple sporting codes. Although no specific clubs were named, the report stated 'the level of suspected use of peptides varies between some sporting codes, however, officials from a club have been identified as administering, via injections and intravenous drips, a variety of substances, possibly including peptides. Moreover, the substances were administered at levels which were possibly in breach of World Anti-Doping Agency (WADA) anti-doping rules.'[16] The report included the following key passages, highlighting the influence of the science field in the sport field:

- 'Widespread use of peptides has been identified or is suspected by the ACC, in a number of professional sporting codes in Australia. Multiple players (in one code) from a number of clubs are suspected of currently using or having previously used peptides.'[17]
- 'An instance of team-based doping orchestrated by some club officials and coaching staff, has also been identified.'[18]
- 'Officials from a club have been identified as administering, via injections and intravenous drips, a variety of substances, possibly including peptides... Moreover, substances were administered at levels which were possibly in breach of WADA anti-doping rules.'[19]
- 'Some medical practitioners have been identified as one of the key conduits through which individuals are obtaining performance and image enhancing drugs (PIEDs).'[20]
- 'The ACC also identified lax and fraudulent prescribing practices by some doctors with links to sporting clubs and anti-ageing clinics. These practices include writing scripts in false names, providing prescriptions without consulting the patient and prescribing hormones without conducting the necessary blood test normally carried out prior to the prescription of these substances.'[21]

- 'Some of these doctors are also implicated in experimenting on players, by providing them with different substances in order to determine the effects on their performance.'[22]
- 'In Australian football codes, sport scientists have gained increasing influence over decision-making within the clubs. Some of these scientists are playing a critical role in pushing legal and regulatory boundaries in relation to sport supplementation programs and medical treatments given to players.'[23]
- 'The ACC has identified specific high-performance staff, sport scientists and coaches within some codes who have condoned and/or orchestrated the administration of prohibited substances and substances not yet approved for human consumption.'[24]
- 'In some cases, peptides and other substances were administered to players without them understanding the nature of the substances and without the knowledge of the team doctor or club medical staff.'[25]
- 'The ACC has identified a range of substances that have limited to no history of use in humans, are not approved for human use or their use is considered "off-label" (page 28). While these substances are not prohibited by WADA, due to a lack of long-term clinical studies on the use of these substances or their "off-label" use, their potential impact on the health of players – both short and long-term – is unknown.'[26]
- 'Sport scientists can play a critical role in taking training programs and the preparation of athletes to the edge of and sometimes beyond, what is permitted by WADA.'[27]

Thus, the science field is clearly exerting an increasing influence on the sport field; and sport scientists are increasingly managing the play element. In some cases, the resulting lack of autonomy and the increased influence have corrupted play and, as shown in the ACC report, are corrupting play.

In addition, the ACC report indicated that the corruption of play is not limited to the influence of the science field but is also linked to organised crime and match fixing:

- 'The presence of organised criminal identities and groups in the performance and image enhancing drugs (PIEDs) market presents a threat to the integrity of Australian professional sport as a direct consequence of the increased likelihood of criminal identities and groups interacting with professional athletes and the potential exploitation of these relationships for criminal purposes.'[28]

- 'Relationships between athletes and organised crime identities can be exploited by criminals to corrupt the athlete... The ACC's 2011 assessment of Threats to the Integrity of Professional Sport in Australia noted that as the amount of money wagered on sport increases, associations with athletes or other individuals with the ability to influence a sporting contest or provide inside information, will be increasingly sought after.'[29]

In their response to the ACC Report, the AFL stated,

> The AFL is strongly supportive of a national match fixing policy as agreed to by federal and state governments in 2011. Last year, the NSW government passed legislation introducing a criminal offence for match fixing with a maximum penalty of ten years' imprisonment and the AFL looks forward to the introduction of similar legislation in other states.
>
> The AFL also recognises that athletes can be vulnerable to 'grooming' by criminals who want to compromise them for match-fixing purposes. The AFL is currently delivering an education program to players and club officials that warns about doping and includes a specific section on the AFL's gambling regulations and the risks that players could face.[30]

Match fixing

According to the *Cambridge Dictionary*, match fixing refers to 'any dishonest activity to make sure that one team wins a particular sport match'.[31] The *Oxford Dictionary* defines it as 'the action or practice of dishonestly determining the outcome of a match before it is played'.[32] Match fixing, like tanking and cheating through the use of prohibited substances, stands in direct opposition to Huizinga's description of play. Individuals or groups who choose to influence the outcomes of contests deliberately by cheating within the sport field corrupt the play element. Thus, match fixing ensures the loss of the innocence of play, whether through the act of not trying to win, the provision of inside information or the manipulation of play to assist criminals in winning money through gambling. Play is no longer free, nor is it spontaneous. Instead, it is staged, manipulated and managed and thereby corrupted.

Match fixing also highlights the negative consequences resulting from the sport field losing its autonomy to the economic field. When the sport field was autonomous, the significance of the contest was restricted to the sport field. Those who won or who were judged the best accumulated social capital through received adulation, respect, satisfaction and honour. Their status and power within other fields of society remained relatively unchanged, nor could individuals outside the sport field utilise play as a means of accumulating capital and power.

Now, the consequence of the contest is no longer felt only within the sport field. Instead, the influence of the economic field and economic capital within the sport field facilitates cheating, thus threatening the integrity of the sport field. The ACC report suggests that organised criminal identities and groups are utilising play and sport as tools to generate economic income through gambling. To ensure their bets pay off, they are influencing players to manipulate contests to effect their desired results, which is usually to lose the match.[33] Although no history of this occurring in the VFL/AFL exists, such corruption has affected cricket, English Premier League soccer and horse racing, among others.

The threat of match fixing in the AFL emerged in 2011 when two Collingwood players were sanctioned for breaking the AFL's anti-gambling rules. Heath Shaw was suspended for fourteen matches (six were subsequently rescinded) and fined $20,000 for placing a $10 bet on teammate and captain Nick Maxwell to kick the first goal of their match against Adelaide. Odds of Maxwell doing so were 100 to 1. A friend of Shaw's also bet on Maxwell. Maxwell was fined $10,000 (with $5,000 later rescinded) because his family placed $85 in bets on him based on Maxwell informing them that he would be starting the round 9 game in the forward line, rather than in his usual defensive position. Although neither Maxwell nor Shaw had bet on the outcome of the game or tried to influence the end result, they still violated rules prohibiting the sharing of sensitive or privileged information, information others could use to make money from play.[34] Although the Shaw–Maxwell suspensions may not be match fixing as such, they still provide an example of the dominating influence of the economic field in transforming play into a money-making tool.

The corruption of play

Today, people gamble thousands of dollars each week on the outcomes of matches or on moments within those matches. Odds on match outcomes are regularly displayed in television broadcast advertisements, integrated into radio broadcasts and shown live on scoreboards at the grounds where the matches are played. Punters can bet on a range of outcomes, including who will win, the margin by which the team will win, who will kick the first goal of the match or quarter, which player will kick the most goals for the match, who will win each quarter of the match and the margin by which the team will win the quarter. According to Huizinga, when utilised for a secondary purpose, such as generating money (for example, gambling), play is less genuine than it was at its origin. If what players, coaches, administrators and supporters are working together to achieve is not real – if it is, in fact, corrupt – it damages the bond generated through play and harms the ability of play to generate communities.

Tanking, the role of science and the issue of gambling illuminate the corruption of play emerging due to the growing influence of the economic field and the loss of autonomy in the sport field. Even though the AFL has not identified any cases of these potential problems yet, the examples discussed highlight the ways in which various levels of management, various departments within the organisation and its clubs and individual players may manipulate the play element to influence contest outcomes. As play is transformed into business, those involved at all levels seem more willing to do whatever it takes to ensure their brands remain attractive to current and potential consumers.

7

Grassroots vs AFL Communities

Australian football encompasses more than the AFL. Football clubs exist at all levels of the sport. Those at the grassroots or local level often reflect the elements of genuine communities more so than the elite clubs do. As discussed earlier, upholding the notions of community is important in ensuring individuals attain a sense of community and, thus, develop as individuals. When money corrupts and transforms communities into tools of the economy – which is what the merger of the economic, media and sport fields is doing – they become weak reflections of what they were originally. The individuals within them, then, are less likely to reach their potential which, in turn, undermines democracy.

Originally, Australian football reflected the people who created it, people who came together to enjoy something in common with others. From that enjoyment, they created football clubs, places in which members felt ownership and made significant contributions to achieve agreed upon goals. Members felt a sense of obligation towards the other members and could influence club decisions. Thus, in their formative years, most VFL clubs reflected true and genuine communities; and their teams played in the true spirit of their clubs.

As the AFL and its clubs transformed into businesses, however, they lost many of the attributes of genuine communities. Thus, the clubs that mirror the characteristics of the founding clubs exist primarily in regional and suburban Australia. Spawned from grassroots efforts, they exist for their members and on behalf of their members. These individuals have ownership in their clubs and actively contribute to the goals and objectives they have outlined together. Therefore, to see the differences in community resulting from the merger of the economic and media fields, we must first examine grassroots football and its communities as they exist currently and then compare them with the AFL and its communities.

Grassroots football

In the foreword to *Footy Town: Stories of Australia's Game*, Paul Daffey notes the active participation of club members at the local, grassroots level of Australian football.[1] Rather than being restricted to mere 'financial members' who contribute monetarily or to members who attend games simply to barrack and cheer, members of these clubs have opportunities to help their clubs operate and function. To illustrate this point, he describes an encounter with Ray Gallagher, president of the Swifts Creek Football Club: 'Ray had just finished a stint on the front gate, while dressed in his footy gear, socks pulled up and jumper tucked in. He was now attending a few last minute items before jogging onto the field to take his place in the back pocket.'[2] Ray was not only a player but also an off-field volunteer.

Daffey also notes that the football club is not only a meeting place and spiritual home for members but also a place where the community, players and supporters gather to 'share appraisals of the game and stories of significant events from the past'.[3] Thus, grassroots clubs bring people together. Submissions to the Parliament of Victoria Rural and Regional Services and Development Committee for its 2004 Inquiry into Country Football highlight this point. Many of these submissions describe the local football club as the heart of the community, the place where club members and locals alike gather in common with others to enjoy the game and make a collective contribution to both their club and their community.[4]

Sometimes, the club is the sole opportunity available, as the submission by Wimmera Regional Sport notes:

> Football also provides the actual opportunity for people to meet and to share memories…and to focus on a positive in their lives… Most clubs host social functions before and after the game. Sometimes that is the only social connection or activity for the local population to engage with.[5]

Tom Hafey, a former VFL player and coach, and champion of grassroots football, observes that football matches may be the only regular social event available to a community:

> I was doing a sportsmen's night down at Portland… An old fellow said to me, "Tommy, since our little football-netball club at Yambuk closed down" – which was five or six years at that stage – "I haven't seen my next-door neighbour. I see his car whizzing down the highway.' The football-netball club used to bring everybody out.[6]

According to Dr R. Moodie of VicHealth,

> Football clubs provide a sense of belonging to the local community for thousands of people as they provide a place to gather and interact with others. This brings people from all walks of life together in supporting a local community actively, which might not happen in any other form. Doctors, farmers, local businesses, tradesmen, police, school teachers might all belong to the football club.[7]

Unfortunately, this point is most starkly realised when football clubs are taken away from the community.

Daffey also discusses his discovery of a community in Western Australia that stimulates the growth of individuals and helps them achieve their potential and develop as members of the community:

> It was at Beacon, in the country, just before the paddocks meet the desert. Every player – no exclusions – who won an award had to say a few words when he went up the front to collect his award. Every player is encouraged to grow.[8]

Of importance here is the concept of active support and participation. A true sense of community exists when members of the club and the community are empowered to come together to contribute actively to reach shared goals. In doing so, citizens feel a sense of obligation towards each other and a sense of fulfilment.

Several of the AFL club members and supporters I interviewed also describe the sense of community they feel as participants in their local clubs. Jeremiah Ryan played football for the Swinburne Razorbacks Amateur Football Club:

Swinburne was a really struggling sort of club for money, sponsorship, for players, for support staff, for everything. I served for two years as president for the club. My secretary and treasurer were both players. The majority of the committee were players. It [the club] was generally driven by the people who wanted to play football... I felt like Swinburne really needed me. Like if myself and maybe two or three other people died in our sleep, the club wouldn't exist the following morning. The people there are still some of my best friends. [I] talk to them regularly. We won the premiership in 2007 and I got a tattoo of the club logo. I felt very, very close to the club.

Fellow Swinburne player Phil Wild shares similar sentiments:

You know the players a lot more intimately at your [local] club and you know them as people... That really means that you have more of a connection with the club...especially where I play at the moment. [At] the Swinburne Footy Club there's a lot of social events and a lot of ties between the guys...it's a really good thing to have.

Each week, Wild spends at least ten hours involved with the club, training with the team, attending to his committee duties and just staying in touch:

Personally I'm on the committee at the moment, so that obviously means I've got a large amount of say in what the actual comings and goings of the club are. I mean, being a university club, we don't have a lot of old boys and so forth, so the people who are on board – the board, the committee – are actually current players. So if there's something that's affecting us and we'd like to change, then we have a very direct ability to change that by changing a part of the way the club operates.

In addition, he plays for the team and attends club social functions: 'And I do it [all] because I love it, of course.'

Wild notes the difference in the sense of community he feels being part of the Swinburne Amateur Football Club compared with his support of the Swans of the AFL:

[It's] that feeling of playing with the guys every week and seeing the results come in and so on and hopefully, towards the end of the year, getting into the finals; it's not something you get in any other part of life...even with the Swans… [T]he Swans won the premiership last year. It was amazing, [but] I don't think that would be as good as if my team, Swinburne, won the premiership as well because you're involved in it a little more closely.

Geelong Cats supporter Kate Withers explains that she feels a different kind of attachment to her local club than she does to her AFL club: 'At a participation level, I feel a certain sense of obligation to my local sporting clubs – they're smaller and rely heavily on the continued investment (financially, emotionally, et cetera) from members.' Because of her involvement with the Olinda Bloods, 'from boundary umpiring as a twelve-year-old girl to now helping out at Auskick', Alanna Ford is also closer to her local club.

The sense of community he found within the four grassroots clubs he'd played for amounted to one thing for Neil Duncan: 'I knew the people and they were the people I wanted to be with.'[9] Michael Westland concurs: '80 per cent of the people I hang around with regularly are from the Northcote Cricket Club and the Swinburne Football Club. And being part of that inner sanctum, you make a generation of friends. And that's what being part of an inner sanctum of a football club is…it's a collection of people with similar beliefs that are choosing to be part of that community…they're the key stakeholders. You know, they invest their time and their emotions in that community.' The level of involvement is also a factor for Scott Hutchins, whose local club is the Swinburne Razorbacks: 'After a game I'd stay at the club on a Saturday night or you'd have functions during the week or a working bee on a Sunday…whereas Geelong, I'd go to the games. I don't go to events outside of football. So I definitely feel much closer ties to the clubs that I've actually been involved in.'

Indeed, when Australian football clubs act autonomously from other more commercial fields of society, they stimulate genuine relationships, community and personal growth. The Associated Judaean Athletic Club (AJAX) is one such club. Founded in 1957 by the Jewish community as a reflection of their shared enthusiasm for Australia's native game, AJAX is part of the Victoria Amateur Football Association (VAFA).[10] Because the members' beliefs, values and personalities define the club, AJAX also reflects the Jewish community. Club historian Barry Markoff notes that although money is not an essential ingredient of the club's survival, any money required to run the club comes through fundraising events, such as barbecues, open to the entire Jewish community, who respond 'by turning up in their droves'.[11] Of greater importance is Markoff's observation that 'the club provided a point of social contact for Jewish immigrants coming to Australia after World War II and the existence of the AJAX Football Club no doubt contributed to a greater acceptance of Jewish people within Australian society'.[12]

According to Andrew Demetriou, former chief executive of the AFL, Australian football is all encompassing and inclusive. It is integrating, accepting and multicultural, transcending class and ethnicity. Although this may be true to some extent within the AFL, it is certainly a prevailing feature of community sport. Here, common, shared and enjoyed pursuits can break down social, cultural, ethnic and gender barriers.[13]

However, the AJAX Football Club proves that this has not always been the case (and still is not). In 1972, religion and Australian football collided. The AJAX Football Club Reserves team qualified for the VAFA Grand Final. The match was to be played on 9 September, which was also Rosh Hashanah, the Jewish New Year celebration, one of the three most sacred days of the Jewish faith. Because playing sport on that day is not permitted in the Jewish faith, AJAX sent a letter to the VAFA and to all the VAFA clubs requesting the match be rescheduled. With the exception of the Marcellin Football Club, neither the VAFA nor its clubs were willing to do so, forcing AJAX to forfeit.[14] When this conflict arose again in 1999, the VAFA did change the date, ensuring that AJAX could play and ultimately showing its recognition and respect for the differing values, spirit and beliefs that shaped VAFA clubs.[15]

AJAX's decision to forfeit in 1972 also illustrates the concept of community in grassroots clubs. The community decided together not to play in the grand final. They decided together to uphold the beliefs, values and personality that characterise their club and its community. Indeed, without those characteristics, the club would not have existed, much less have qualified for the grand final.

Today, clubs at the grassroots level are still generating and stimulating cultures and communities that reflect Huizinga's concept of authentic culture and mirror what the VFL was as its founding. Indeed, many of the grassroots football clubs in the country and suburban areas appear to be integral parts of cultural life within their communities just as the original VFL clubs were.[6]

The future of grassroots football

Of more importance, however, is that the play element of these grassroots clubs still provides a sense of enjoyment for their players and supporters. It still empowers them to come together to enjoy something in common with others and to engage actively with their fellow members to contribute to the goals and objectives of the club.[17] Thus, members feel both a sense of ownership of their club and, through their active engagement, a sense of self-growth.

Nevertheless, even though these football clubs mirror many of the original foundations of the VFL clubs, the path the VFL/AFL has taken is a stark reminder of where suburban and country football leagues may be headed. Imagining these clubs will ever be as structured, organised and commercial as the AFL may be difficult; but money is already infiltrating the playing lists of many of these country clubs. For these teams, economic capital is becoming the determining factor of team success.

As economic capital becomes a driving factor in the play performance of teams, country football leagues are transforming into semi-professional businesses providing employment for their players. According to Alomes,

> Footy is played for love – but, like some marriages, also for money. Even in the amateurs, coaches can receive five figure sums and rumours abound of contra-deals that attract top players who still play under the hat of amateur status… Money matters in the semi-professional, if part-time, culture of local footy.[18]

One example of this shift is the Ovens and Murray Football League in northern Victoria. From 2009 to 2014, only two teams played in the grand final: the Albury Tigers and the Yarrawonga Pigeons. These two clubs have also reportedly paid players substantially more than their rivals. Such an outcome can only mean these two clubs have relatively more economic capital at their disposal to recruit the best available talent to ensure they win far more often than not.[19]

In terms of player payments, former AFL players joining these grassroots clubs can earn sums of up to $70,000 a year. This is especially true for those serving as playing coaches. Top players can earn $400 to $500 (or more) per game. Some country footballers are already being paid $60,000 to $70,000 a year, which is more than the average individual wage in Australia ($57,980).[20] Thus, 'Money…makes the local footy world go round.'[21]

Just as being paid to play has altered the play element and community in the AFL, so too does paying players at the grassroots level, as Joshua Forte reveals in his description of how this changed his experience in playing for a country grassroots club:

> When I was eighteen, nineteen, realising it was not just a result on the line, [that] there was also money, selfishness certainly crept in and football [lost] its innocence. There's nothing better than running out there when I was seventeen and eighteen; there was just a joy to be playing in front of such a big crowd. It could've been 1,000 people, but that's such a big crowd and it's exciting and it's terrific. And then when you do get the money – of course, I don't think effort dropped off – but mentally, I was like, 'Look, if we do lose this, I'm driving back up the highway with a few hundred dollars, back to Melbourne. I'll get over it a bit quicker.' But losses when I wasn't getting paid, living at home, used to really eat away at me; but I think that financial certainty softened the blow.

Forte also notes that play became much more serious:

> Of course, [getting paid meant] a lot of added pressure, but I like that. I certainly didn't shy away from it, but that added pressure and your family's expectations as well – because they understand this is a club you grew up in – they don't want you to hold that club to ransom.

As the influence of the economic field grows, so too will the consequences. On field, winning will become more important and players more restricted. Play will be measured and increasingly characterised by structures, rules, set plays, planning, statistics, efficiency and seriousness instead of by creativity, spontaneity, freedom and fun. Off field, not even these vibrant suburban, regional and rural football communities are completely shielded from or autonomous from, the economic field. Many country football clubs have already merged with others around them or have ceased to exist because of changing regional landscapes. Where locals born and raised in the community were once likely to become leaders in their communities and to play or volunteer for their club, now they are more likely to move to cities to find employment as soon as they finish school. Thus, these clubs are battling to field teams to play and to find members to volunteer their time to contribute actively to their club.[22] In addition, these clubs will no longer engage their members as much as they once did to contribute actively to generate the necessary, though modest, revenue streams the clubs require. They will supplant activities such as the barbecues held by AJAX in favour of financial donations in the form of sponsorships from local businesses. Thus, these clubs will begin restricting the active participation of their members to financial transactions, much like the AFL.[23]

Yet the sense of community that once defined the VFL still flickers in these grassroots clubs. Despite the strong foothold the economic field appears to be gaining in local, community, grassroots clubs, they still remain closer to the purpose and traditions of the country's original football clubs than does the AFL.

The AFL and community

The AFL and its eighteen clubs continue to be active in their communities, although much of what they do may be categorised as public relations. Players visit hospitals, schools and country football clubs; assist in raising awareness of significant social issues; and participate in fundraising for charity organisations. In 2015, AFL players and clubs reached 467,105 students across Australia. They reached another 182,927 primary school-aged children through their Auskick program, which helped increase total domestic participation in Australian football to 1,247,575 individuals. The AFL has also developed programs to engage and develop youth, such as NAB AFL Auskick, the Sport Ready Trainee Program and the AFL Foundation and community camps. In 2015, through AFL community camps, AFL teams combined to visit all the Australian states and territories, a total of 562 primary and secondary schools and raised more than $66,700 for junior football and community projects. The AFL also engages with other community groups through either developing or supporting Indigenous programs, youth causes, women's organisations, health awareness initiatives, employment programs and similar initiatives.[24] In recent years, this has included the explosion of the number of women and girls playing football, which reached over 300,000 in 2015.[25]

Each club within the AFL contributes to its community through either initiating or supporting local programs and causes. In 2012, the Essendon Football Club announced their community engagement vision was to

> become the benchmark by making a real difference. We aim to be the best sporting organisation from a community perspective in Australia. This will be achieved through our community programs and activities, strong and lasting partnerships and living our own values. We must be genuine in our desire to make a real and significant difference in the community.[26]

To achieve this vision, the club developed and supported several organisations, programs and initiatives within both the broader community and their grassroots community:

- The club partnered or led in nineteen youth, school, multicultural, Indigenous and community programs in 2015.
- The club helped the Cancer Council of Victoria raise in excess of $1 million over the last four years, including $750,000 from its 2011 Windy Hill Relay for Life.
- The club established a multicultural school program to engage students of diverse backgrounds in Australian football while promoting cultural diversity. In 2015, the program engaged in excess of 2,500 students in

Essendon's traditional grassroots community, Melbourne's north-west suburbs.[27]

According to the official club website, Essendon continues to be a fundamental stimulant of communities: 'Sporting clubs at all levels play a significant role in our community. They make a substantial contribution to the fabric of society by providing a focus for the community. They are places where people congregate and become connected to one another.'[28] This sounds remarkably like Huizinga's description of what a sporting club is when play is at its purest and most genuine and is autonomous from the influence of economic capital and the media.

The play element in the AFL unites diverse people. At football matches, men, women and children of the various religions, races and cultures that comprise Australian society sit together, enjoying the game together. Their connection is based upon appreciation and passion for the game, which they share and enjoy equally, regardless of social status, wealth or associated power. Thus, Australian football can be a great equaliser and binding force in society.

Yet, despite the involvement of both the AFL and its clubs in their respective communities, their engagement does not appear to be a genuine source of stimulus for their communities. Clubs such as Essendon do make very real and significant contributions through their many community partnerships and initiatives, but these are separate from the play element, not a result of it. They contribute as organisations and businesses to and within their communities, which is distinctly different from the play element stimulating a community from the bottom up. Essendon contributes through lending brand support, monetary assistance, reputation and the popularity of the game. However, these kinds of contributions should not be confused with play naturally creating the community and the culture of the community, as it once did.

At its purest, play engages citizens to participate in something fun and spontaneous, something unattached to economic capital and quite separate from the real and ordinary world. Play enables participants to act without restriction because the sport field is autonomous. Players can show their whole selves, act with freedom and abandon and form meaningful and lasting relationships with fellow participants within the sport field. Thus, the play element stimulates, builds and binds the community.

The engagement the AFL and its clubs now have with their communities is distinctly different. It is participation within the community, not creation of community. In those instances when they do create communities, they do so through partnering with other organisations or by building something separate from their clubs through leveraging the popularity of their brands and play packages. The aim of Essendon Football Club's Multicultural Schools Program, for example, is to unite people of diverse backgrounds through a program quite separate from the play element within the club.[29] Thus, even though the AFL and its clubs establish and fund initiatives which have positive influences and impacts on society, these initiatives are manufactured, not engendered, the result of the clubs acting as businesses.

The AFL and its clubs also view their communities as markets of consumers. Getting out into the community is simply another way of selling the AFL and club brands. AFL players are contracted to appear at AFL and community events and to visit schools, hospitals and junior football clubs, all to promote their football clubs and the AFL brand. Thus, they are not engaging with their communities freely, even if they enjoy doing so, because the underlying reasons for their engagement are related to economic capital. This is far different from engagement resulting from play that is autonomous and unaffected by money.

The community in the grandstands is also quite different, appearing to be more momentary than enduring. Supporters still meet and greet their fellow fans in the grandstands where they barrack, cheer, curse, vent their frustrations and share somewhat emotional experiences. However, after coming together for two hours to appreciate play in common with one another, they go their separate ways. They do not return to the social rooms of their football clubs to discuss their communities, important issues and matters of interest or concern, all of which occurred when the play element was part of folk culture.

Even the viewing experience for football fans has been commodified, influenced by economic capital. As if to mirror society, AFL grandstands are structured in relation to social status: Seats at the very top of the stadium are the least expensive; seats near the bottom, close to the action, are more expensive. Middle-level seats are even more expensive, often equipped with television sets and cushioned seats. Corporate boxes host society's leading businesses and business associates. As Peter Di Sisto explains, 'There is definite inequality in the grandstands. The rich sit in the best seats with the best memberships and even in corporate boxes. Those that cannot afford it sit way up the back of the grandstands.'

Although not yet as severely commercialised and commodified as play in other sport leagues around the world (such as the English Premier League), play in the AFL merely simulates what it was when the game was invented. The AFL clubs still show elements of evenness, fairness, equality and egalitarianism; and, along with the clubs, the organisation does make genuine efforts to influence communities positively. There even exists some sense that players still play with an element of mateship, togetherness and community spirit.

Unlike grassroots football clubs, however, community engagement in the AFL is somewhat manufactured. It is not a natural evolution of participating in play. Thus, although the AFL and its clubs participate in their communities and do influence them, they do not seem to create communities or to bind them together.

8

From Communities to Markets

As we have seen, play at the founding of Australian football stimulated communities and community experiences. Citizens enjoyed coming together to play or to watch those who played and were largely responsible for the founding and development of Australian football clubs. Club members were the owners and custodians of the game, which represented the collective will, wants, lifestyle and personality of the people. Thus, they were the number one stakeholders of the game.

We have also seen that the game increasingly reflects the dominating influence of the economic and media fields and the neoliberal ideals which appear to dominate most fields of society, even in local grassroots teams, albeit to a lesser extent. How did this come about? Why have we sacrificed genuine community for market share and increased revenues? To understand the changes that have occurred since the formal introduction of the AFL, we must understand the philosophy undergirding them.

The rise of neoliberalism in Australia

Neoliberalism is the philosophy that money and markets can always do everything better than governments, bureaucracies and the law. Over the last three decades, the transformation in Australia effected by this philosophy may be seen as the triumph of economic rationalism, the doctrine that to organise society more rationally all social forms and all social relations should be based on market principles and be subject to market imperatives.[1] As such, new means and methods of making money have spawned in almost all forms and facets of Australian life.

The dominance of neoliberalism in Australia has stretched well beyond the boundaries of economics, politics and business to become one of the most prominent and defining features of its culture, affecting the way Australians consume and interact with their culture and, indeed, with each other.

This philosophy came to prominence in the late 1970s in response to stagnating economic growth, stagflation and increasing government budget deficits. After a generation of Keynesian economic rule based on macro-economic policy and the importance of government in stimulating economic activity and growth, Western leaders began placing a greater emphasis on micro-economic reform and market-based imperatives, which are fundamentally the characteristics of neoliberalism.[2] At the core of the neoliberal agenda is the unwavering belief that, when able to act freely without government interference, the market will be self-regulating and produce the most efficient, productive and effective economic outcomes, thus creating higher quality products and services at a more efficient cost.[3] This will, in turn, lead to higher consumer demand, increased profits and increased employment opportunities.

Most neoliberals are steadfastly united in their belief that government should minimise its spending and interference in the operation of the market and that the private sector should be allowed to act autonomously. In doing so, the private sector will result in better and more efficient outcomes than the government will ever produce.

Thus, neoliberal governments, especially those of Ronald Reagan in America and Margaret Thatcher in Britain, began implementing strict neoliberal policy, which, to differing degrees, much of the West followed, including Australia. The dominant features across most neoliberal economies in the 1980s were increased privatisation, deregulation of previously government-regulated sectors and the reduced role and spending of government in the market. These were the fundamental cornerstones of ensuring consistent and genuine economic growth.[4]

However, the neoliberal policies of privatisation, deregulation and reduced government spending were in opposition to the principles and government agenda to which Australia had committed in shaping democracy at its founding in 1901. In establishing a true and genuine democracy, Australian leaders believed that the state was responsible for ensuring citizens could act freely in common with others, enabling them to strive actively for shared and common goals.[5] Social welfare programs were fundamentally important in ensuring all citizens had appropriate access to the resources considered necessary to engage and participate freely in community life. Therefore, they strongly advocated government spending on welfare and the redistribution of wealth to those who needed it most. By doing this, not only individuals but also the broader society would benefit, evolving and developing into genuine communities.[6]

The rapid acceleration of the neoliberal framework throughout the 1980s and 1990s, matched with unpresented economic and private sector growth, encouraged entrepreneurism. Industries which had always generated some level of money became fully embedded in the neoliberal mantra of producing profit. This included sporting industries such as the AFL. Nothing was off limits or out of bounds; everything that could be used to generate profit was utilised. Even industries which were not fully privately owned or did not function to profit implemented neoliberal styles of management. This ensured the principles of efficiency, productivity and profit became the norm in all facets of life. Indeed, the global market and its neoliberal policies were considered inevitable and irresistible. They were just 'common sense'. Throughout the 1990s, the AFL and its clubs increasingly reflected this business model.

The dominance of neoliberal policy, along with a seemingly blind faith in self-regulating markets, led to extremely uncertain times in the 2000s. The deregulation of the finance sector, the relaxing of many prudent lending and borrowing regulations and the encouragement of entrepreneurism through neoliberal policy stimulated an unforeseen frenzy of financial lending and borrowing. Many Western governments lifted interest rate ceilings. They also removed restrictions on foreign financial organisations entering domestic markets,[7] believing that competition within the finance sector would result in more attractive services for the private sector, international investors and burgeoning entrepreneurs.⁸ Although this worked for most of the two preceding decades, it had come with high risk.

The real estate boom in the United States and Australia in the 1990s and early 2000s led many corporate and individual investors to borrow large sums of money against inflated real estate values, resulting in a massive transfer of wealth and income to the financial sector.⁹ Banks borrowed from their competitors with the intention of lending that money at higher interest rates. As levels of foreign investment increased, which had been occurring steadily since the advent of globalisation, banks and other financial institutions competed to offer both domestic and foreign borrowers the most attractive services at the most competitive rates. In doing so, however, they forgot the prudent rules of lending.

These practices came to a head during the real estate bust in the United States, which reached a crisis point in 2008. The severe drop in real estate values meant a significant decline in the overall value of bank assets, which led to an equally significant drop in market shares. Many borrowers were left unable to pay back their loans. Subsequently, banks were unable to meet their debt obligations. Even when they reclaimed assets from bankrupt clients, they were well short of what they were owed and, indeed, what they themselves owed.¹⁰

With many financial organisations declaring bankruptcy, governments in Europe and the United States expressed their dismay by imposing far stricter restrictions on borrowing and lending than the banks had imposed in the free market. Because of these restrictions, companies which had relied on accessing credit to create investment or to pay their creditors could no longer obtain bank financing. In addition, many large multinational corporations also defaulted on their loans and declared bankruptcy. The severely reduced financial investment resulted in plummeting job creation. As unemployment figures rose, economic activity reached the crisis point.¹¹ Thus, the financial crisis became an economic crisis of global proportions due to the interconnectedness of most Western economies.

In Australia, the Labor government led by Kevin Rudd chose to interfere in the free market, convinced it needed correcting. The Australian prime minister and his treasurer, Wayne Swan, chose to stimulate economic activity by distributing one-off payments and encouraging citizens to spend those payments in the market to sustain adequate levels of consumer spending and economic activity. Thus, the Rudd government significantly reduced the effects of the global financial crisis.[12]

However, defendants of neoliberalism and sceptics among the Australian electorate met the Rudd government's decision with extreme hostility. They perceived the government spending as reckless and irresponsible. So used to the neoliberal style of management were the Australian electorate that instead of praising the Rudd government for keeping the economy largely removed from the effects of the global financial crisis, they criticised it for generating a budget deficit. Thus, the Australian community received the Rudd government's step away from neoliberal principles towards Keynesian economic principles with lukewarm enthusiasm, seeing neoliberal ideals as the natural and normal way of life. The changing focus of the Western world's political and economic ideology had a significant impact on the sports field, including at the top level of Australian football.

The increasing influence of economic capital in the VFL/AFL

The period from the late 1970s through the 1980s was one of great change in the VFL. As the Australian economic landscape began to embrace neoliberalism and economic rationalist objectives, so too did most elite sporting organisations. As many of the key participants within the sport field began placing greater emphasis on the importance and significance of economic capital, the VFL began to function as a commercial business, mirroring most other fields of society.

One consequence of this was the overriding importance of money for the players, coaches, clubs and league compared with the importance of community. Of particular importance in the VFL was the accumulation of economic capital through the commercialisation of the game, which highlighted the increased role of the media in selling the VFL brand to new markets.[13] By packaging and selling their product in these new markets, the VFL could attract higher television audiences and, thereby, increase their revenue. Such commercial benefits were the apparent factor in the relocation of the South Melbourne Football Club to Sydney and the merger of Fitzroy with Brisbane and its subsequent relocation to Brisbane.

The move to Sydney

South Melbourne was one of Australia's first Australian football clubs. Created as the Cecil Football Club in 1874, it changed its name to the South Melbourne Football Club to reflect its South Melbourne origins. The club enjoyed success in the VFA competition between 1881 and 1890 but, at the end of the 1896 season, joined seven other clubs in breaking away to form the VFL. The club won three premierships between 1909 and 1933, and enjoyed its most successful period from 1933 through 1936, during which it played in four consecutive grand finals. This success was largely due to an influx of money from fundraising efforts undertaken to recruit quality players from interstate teams, most of which were in Western Australia. Thus, as early as the 1930s, the link between economic capital and the sport field was evident in on-field success. From 1946 until 1981, however, the club only made the VFL finals series twice, both during the 1970s. Their on-field record was the worst in the VFL competition.[14]

South Melbourne's lack of on-field success resulted in something of an off-field crisis. Their supporter base had been declining since the 1940s. Many once loyal fans had moved from the community to the outer suburbs and had stopped attending South Melbourne matches.[15] In addition, prospective sponsors were unwilling to form commercial partnerships with a football club commonly associated with losing. A dwindling supporter base coupled with a lack of sponsors resulted in steadily accumulating debt from the 1940s to the beginning of the 1980 season. Reportedly, by 1981, the Swans had recorded operating losses of at least $150,000 per year for the last five years.[16]

The South Melbourne Football Club's inability to generate revenue and to accumulate economic capital precipitated the business decisions club officials began to make to transform the club into a viable, profitable entity. In July 1981, the administration and board of directors announced their proposal to the VFL to move their home and away games, abandoning Lake Oval, their ground in South Melbourne for the last 108 years: All away games were to be played in Sydney; all home games at VFL Park in Waverley. The rationale for this change was the board of directors' belief that the move to Sydney would turn an operating loss of $180,000 in 1980 to a profit in 1982.[17] To justify their decision to their loyal South Melbourne community and the broader VFL community, many of whom were battling to come to terms with the increasing role of economic capital in the game, the South Melbourne board developed an economic rationalist framework. Journalists covering both the issue and the VFL used this framework to legitimise the economic case for moving to Sydney.[18]

The VFL supported South Melbourne's proposal to relocate half of their games to Sydney. A significant aspect of the league's financial and economic strategy was to expand its product into the northern markets of Australia, especially into Sydney and Brisbane, by selling to new markets and potential revenue sources. Interestingly, the players who represented the South Melbourne Football Club and community enthusiastically endorsed the board's proposal. Their reason was largely the same as that of the other key participants in the evolving sport field: money. Many of the players either had not been paid their full wages or could not demand the amount of money they might attract at a more financially secure club.[19] Player payments had always been a part of the game; but in the late 1970s and the 1980s, the emphasis was on rewarding players financially for providing a form of entertainment. In conjunction with that emphasis, players were increasingly used as tools to attract consumers to the VFL brand. After all, the players were the star attractions of the show. Thus, the South Melbourne players exemplified the mind set of players within the VFL at that time: They no longer competed for capital autonomous to other fields of society; instead, they struggled for economic capital, which provided them with power, success, recognition and financial security. These, in turn, augmented the neoliberal characteristics of the economic field in transforming the sport field.

The play–money–media cycle was fundamental to the VFL's national expansion strategy. With the assistance of the media, the VFL used the introduction of the Sydney and Brisbane teams to expand its product into Australia's northern markets. There, the organisation could market, package, promote and sell its product to new consumers to generate larger television audiences for VFL games. Larger television audiences in the southern and northern states meant the VFL could demand higher payments for broadcast rights, thus increasing revenues. Again, money was the underlying determinant of activity within the VFL.

Despite the endorsement by many of the key participants, the South Melbourne community and supporter base fought to keep what they believed was theirs. Over one thousand South Melbourne supporters protested at the Lake Oval in July 1981, trying to ensure their club remained in their community. At the same time, a group of South Melbourne supporters formed Keep South at South, a group that petitioned against the South Melbourne board's decision. These individuals felt genuine ownership of their club and did not see the move as a business decision but as the South Melbourne board taking their club away from them. The petition generated 183 supporter signatures, enough to force an extraordinary general meeting, which was held on 22 September 1981.[20]

According to Ron Reed of the *Herald*, 'Although South Melbourne's extraordinary meeting was an emotional occasion, where much mention was made of things like loyalty and tradition, the argument boiled down, purely and simply, to the most necessary of evils, money.'[21] When the issue came to a vote, 80 per cent of the members voted against the proposal. However, as Reed noted, 'a couple of blokes in red jumpers selling raffle tickets was not enough to put goals on the scoreboard'.[22] Despite the support of 80 per cent of the South Melbourne members, Keep South at South did not have the support of either the players or the VFL administration.[23]

When discussions between Keep South at South and the players disintegrated, the players boycotted training. In November 1981, seventeen South Melbourne players issued the club a summons claiming the organisation owed them more than $79,000 because they had not been paid since round 10 of the previous season. According to Mike Sheahan, 'It was time for emotion to make way for common sense', which meant placing economic stability ahead of tradition, history and the South Melbourne community.[24] In December, the VFL intervened and merged the South Melbourne board of directors with the Keep South at South board. The league then donated $400,000 to the club to ensure the players received all that they were owed under the condition that the administration commit to playing in Sydney for the next two years. Thus, for the first time in the history of the VFL, the players and their desire to accumulate economic capital determined the future of a football club.

Eventually, the economic field and the importance of economic capital prevailed. In 1982, the club played all its home games in Sydney.[25] In 1983, the Swans permanently relocated to Sydney. This relocation made clear that the number one stakeholders were now those who could generate revenue and confirmed the transformation of the game into a business whose economic rationale and neoliberal objectives have determined the direction of the game ever since.[26]

Continued expansion

The VFL introduced two new teams in 1987: the West Coast Eagles, based in Perth and the Brisbane Bears. The introduction of the Western Australian team seemed a natural evolution because Western Australians had been playing, following and supporting Australian football for over a hundred years. The introduction of the Queensland team appeared less natural, however. The Brisbane Bears was not a grassroots club formed by the Brisbane community, which preferred rugby league and rugby union to Australian football. Instead, the club was a manufactured creation to expand the VFL into new markets to attract new supporters and larger television audiences and was partly owned by controversial and flash businessman Christopher Skase.

To reflect their growing national reach and to state their intention to expand across the entire nation, the VFL changed its name to the Australian Football League (AFL) before the 1990 season. In 1991, the AFL introduced the Adelaide Crows into the competition. In 1995, it introduced a second Western Australian team, the Fremantle Dockers. Two years later, the Port Adelaide Power joined the AFL.[27] However, the addition of all three teams was apparently as much the result of grassroots efforts as of the AFL's economic rationalist model of expanding into new markets. Supporters of Australian football in these communities had been lobbying for representation in the elite competition for decades.

The Fitzroy–Brisbane merger

At the same time that the AFL was developing its expansion strategy, however, many of its foundation clubs in Victoria were struggling with the economic demands of the new business model they had been forced to adopt. In 1996, for example, while West Coast attracted 27,681 members and the Adelaide Crows attracted 42,483, Fitzroy could attract only 7,628, in part due to the competition among nine teams for supporters within one city.[28] While West Coast and Adelaide spent the income generated from their membership sales to improve their clubs, Fitzroy fought to survive. The club's on-field performance reflected this battle as well, with Fitzroy winning only three matches in their final two seasons.[29]

Like South Melbourne, the Fitzroy Football Club had a long history dating to its founding in 1883. Representing the Melbourne inner suburb of Fitzroy, the Lions were one of the foundation clubs of the VFL and won eight premierships between 1898 and 1944. Like South Melbourne, Fitzroy struggled to accumulate its share of economic capital in the crowded Melbourne market. The lack of economic capital required to maintain and upgrade their home ground had already forced the club to move from Brunswick Street Oval in 1966. From 1984 until 1996, the club had four different home grounds, none of which were in Fitzroy. In 1978, the club reported a loss of $120,000, not an insignificant amount at that time. By July 1980, Fitzroy was 'technically bankrupt' and the board of directors began considering alternative, economically 'sound and responsible' options, including relocating to Sydney; but the members defeated that proposal.[30]

Unable to meet their financial obligations, the board of directors began considering merging their club with Melbourne. Members and fans from both clubs reacted hostilely to this proposal and subsequently defeated it. With that defeat, Fitzroy president Leon Wiergard stated the club had only a 50 per cent chance of surviving in its own right.[31]

Again, the VFL intervened, proposing to relocate Fitzroy to Brisbane as part of its expansion strategy. The Fitzroy board initially accepted the proposal, but the relocation fell through when the club gained Hecron as a corporate sponsor and received enough money to remain in Melbourne.[32] Financial solvency lasted only three years, however.

Again unable to meet its financial obligations, Fitzroy agreed to merge with the struggling Footscray Football Club. This merger also disintegrated when the Footscray community, led by supporter Irene Chatfield, raised enough economic capital to keep the club alive. Footscray's survival, however, came with a cost. To increase its marketability beyond its original community, the club had to change its name to the Western Bulldogs in 1997. Although the name suggested that the club represented the West, not just Footscray, supporters offered little resistance because they preferred keeping their club to either merging it with another or relocating.[33]

Despite this, Fitzroy continued to flail. Only economic capital could ensure their independence and keep them in Melbourne and the Fitzroy community could not contribute enough to ensure the club's financial security. Thus, the community had to relinquish its role as the number one stakeholder in the club. Other participants who had a better understanding of the economic field and its neoliberal characteristics and greater abilities to accumulate the needed economic capital became the decision makers.

In June 1996, the Nauru Insurance Company, a creditor of the Fitzroy Football Club, appointed their own administrator, Michael Brennan, to administer the financial affairs of the club and to ensure repayment of the $1.25 million Nauru had loaned the club. This loan was only part of a reported overall debt of $4.5 million owed to various creditors. In July, the Fitzroy Football Club and the North Melbourne Football Club agreed on terms for merging. However, discussions stalled over emotional issues based on history and tradition, such as the name for the new club, the colours players would wear and the team nickname. Some substantive issues were also unresolved, such as the structuring of the new board of directors and the number of players from each team to remain on the merged team's playing list. In the interim, the AFL and the majority of its clubs voted to merge Fitzroy and the Brisbane Bears to form the Brisbane Lions.[34]

North Melbourne officials claimed the AFL endorsed the merger as part of its strategy to create an attractive product for the Queensland market. However, according to Noel Gordon, the Brisbane president at the time, the merger was the result of Brisbane having a superior knowledge of economic capital: 'While they [Fitzroy and North Melbourne] might have agreed between themselves what they wanted to do, there were certain [financial] obligations Fitzroy had to honour…such as the debt to the Nauruan Government.'[35]

The Fitzroy merger highlights again the dominating influence of the economic field and neoliberalism on decisions made by key participants in the VFL/AFL. These individuals shaped the field, augmenting the economic structure of the AFL and ultimately transforming it into a business. Communities had little control over the future of their clubs. No amount of passion, tradition or loyalty could save them. Only economic capital, in the form of money, could prevent clubs from merging or relocating. When supporters could no longer provide enough economic capital, they had to relinquish their place as number one stakeholders to those who could provide the industry with money.

The Tasmanian bid

The VFL/AFL's desire to expand the game into the northern markets was also a key factor in awarding the league's seventeenth and eighteenth club licenses: the Gold Coast in 2009 and Greater Western Sydney in 2010. That the AFL looked beyond the traditional heartland of Australian football to Queensland and New South Wales was far from surprising given its commitment to reaching new consumers and increasing television audiences. However, the placement of clubs in markets with relatively little affinity for Australian football appears especially stark in light of the rejection of Tasmania's bid for an AFL team.

Tasmania has had a history of playing and watching Australian football dating to the 1860s. It was the 'first state outside of Victoria to play the game, with football clubs established in New Town, Derwent and Stowell in and around 1864'.[36] The Tasmanian Football League was created in 1879 in the Hobart community and the Northern Tasmanian Football Association was formed in 1886. Not only has Tasmanian football generated many VFL and AFL footballers, including Darrel Baldock, Royce Hart, Peter Hudson, Ian Stewart, Alistair Lynch and Matthew Richardson; but its participation rate has also been higher than any other state or territory in Australia with the exception of the Northern Territory, which also does not have an AFL team.[37]

Throughout the last century, the VFL/AFL has played many exhibition and home and away matches in Tasmania. The AFL has even encouraged Victorian clubs experiencing financial difficulties to turn to Tasmania to attract support. North Melbourne and Hawthorn have availed themselves of this opportunity, marketing themselves as 'Tasmania's teams' to ensure their brands are attractive to the Tasmanian market. Hawthorn has been playing home games in Launceston since 2003 and is contracted to do so until at least 2017, based on a deal with the Tasmanian government worth $17 million over five years. North Melbourne has been playing three home games at Bellerive Oval in Hobart since 2012.[38] Thus, Tasmania's relationship with the AFL has largely been based on money, with AFL clubs looking to the Tasmanian market as a means of increasing their revenues and membership base. In 2015, for example, Hawthorn had over 8,900 Tasmanian-based members, who generated approximately $1 million in revenue, in addition to the approximately $3.4 million received from the Tasmanian government.[39]

Before this, however, Tasmania developed a proposal for its own AFL team in 2008. Tasmania, It's Time, a website advocating for such a team, listed the following ten points as reasons the AFL should approve the bid:[40]

1. We've been playing footy in this state since 1864 – surely our long and proud footy heritage means we should at least get a look in.
2. We've proven that Tasmania can produce AFL stars of the highest calibre. Some of the great names in Australian football have come from Tasmania: Stewart, Baldock, Hart, Hudson, Eade, Lynch and Richardson to name a few.
3. We're a footy state – our participation rates are amongst the highest in the country.
4. We've got great facilities and Aurora Stadium is already up to AFL standards.
5. We have the economy and population to sustain an AFL team.
6. We believe a Tasmanian AFL team would attract strong corporate support and investment into the state.
7. We can compete with the best in the country – just look at our cricket team.
8. We want one. There is overwhelming community support both locally and nationally for a Tasmanian team.
9. We'd support the team and go to the games – live AFL attracts crowds of between 15,000 and 20,000 people per match and a Tassie team of our own would attract even more.
10. It's not truly a national competition without a Tasmanian team.

The website also posted testimonials from influential Tasmanians. One such individual, AFL sport commentator Tim Lane, states,

> A Tasmanian team in the AFL is the island state's football entitlement and its only appropriate destiny. It would unify the island state like nothing before it and bring a bold new story to a vibrant sporting competition. Tasmania in the AFL is an idea whose time has come.[41]

According to Tasmanian VFL football great Peter Hudson,

> Nobody could question that Tasmania is more than entitled to a team in the AFL. This is overwhelmingly supported by the number of players that Tasmania has produced to play AFL football at the highest level and also Tasmania is one of the foundation States of our great game. Tasmania deserves this opportunity.[42]

The Tasmanian bid reflected the old-fashioned grassroots and community sentiments of participation, history, passion and the state's ability to generate elite level footballers. The bid also acknowledged the influence of the economic field and the necessity of attracting members and corporate sponsorship: Had the AFL approved the bid, Tasmania would have had to accumulate at least $30 million in revenue. At the time of the bid, Tasmania had already confirmed $4 million per year from corporate sponsor Mars. The rest of the revenue was to be raised through memberships and other corporate sponsorships, including naming rights sponsors, ten second-tier sponsors and one hundred business supporters.[43]

Despite the community's passion and commitment, the AFL rejected Tasmania's bid. Although the commitment between the AFL and Tasmanian government for two AFL clubs to play in Tasmania until at least 2021 might have compromised Tasmania's bid for their own AFL team, the reason for the rejection was more likely a matter of media audiences. In simple terms, by increasing audiences across the country and by attracting new viewers from new markets, the television broadcasters and the AFL could expect increased revenues and profits. Tasmanians have played Australian football for more than 150 years and have followed VFL and AFL football for almost as long. They already have traditional allegiances to Victorian clubs, many of which go back for generations. Therefore, even without a Tasmanian team, Tasmanians will continue to consume play in the AFL and watch it on television. Indeed, Tasmania is already a captive market, consuming the AFL, watching it on TV and contributing to the revenue flows of both the AFL and its media broadcasters. Thus, the Tasmanian bid for an AFL team was most likely never part of the AFL's strategic, financial and commercial plans. As a result, however, grass roots participation in Tasmania was actually under threat.

Although the AFL and AFL historians offered other reasons to explain the failure of the Tasmanian bid, most of them were also based on matters concerning economic capital. However, as noted previously, 'If the AFL really wanted to love the game…they'd probably have a team in Tasmania.'[44]

Markets vs communities

The transformation of the AFL and its clubs from communities sharing the common goal of coming together to enjoy playing football and being with one another to businesses whose bottom line is an ever-growing profit margin mirror the tenets of neoliberalism. Clubs that began as grassroots creations reflecting their respective communities have become markets, the game sold as entertainment to consumers who relate to their teams through their consumption of display. These consumers play no significant role in the formation of their clubs, nor do they create clubs within their communities. Instead, the AFL develops clubs for television. Any reflections of their communities or cultures in the image of these clubs are the result of the media and marketing fields, which manufacture and contrive them to market their products to the consumers.

The merger of the sport and economic fields has precipitated the push for capital heteronomous to – that is, different from – the sport field. As participants realise the benefits of accumulating economic capital to succeed within the field, this drive for money has redefined the sport field and further strengthened the influence of the economic field.

Fans and supporters also recognise the link between money and winning. To prosper both on and off the field, their football clubs must generate economic capital: Money enables teams to win and winning assists clubs in generating money. As Geelong member Scott Hutchins states,

> It definitely helps to be a strong club [financially]. You can employ a greater number of coaching staff, have more sought after coaching staff and obviously that goes to the back room people like sport scientists. And particularly now with free agents…the bigger clubs are more likely to command more free agents and bigger names.

Michael Westland, an Essendon supporter and member of the AFL, sees an intrinsic link between economic capital and on-field success: 'You would have to assume and you would annually observe that the teams with more (money), with better facilities…are generally at the top for longer.'

This link is also one factor in the expansion decisions of the AFL. The organisation manufactured the Greater Western Sydney Giants and the Gold Coast Suns to expand into the markets of New South Wales and Queensland, despite the communities in these areas not having a traditional love or passion for Australian football. The AFL rejected the Tasmanian bid because it already had the allegiance of the fans and was already generating revenues from them, revenues that were not likely to expand to any great degree with the addition of an AFL club.

Thus, communities have given way to markets. The influence of the economic and media fields has elevated key financial contributors to the status of number one stakeholders in the AFL, who make decisions based on the ever-growing need for additional economic capital. Club members, supporters and fans no longer have meaningful ownership of either their clubs or the game. What once was a game owned and enjoyed by community members is now a form of entertainment designed to generate revenue. As such, the AFL mirrors most other fields in its pursuit of money at the expense of community.

9

Members, Supporters and Fans: Views from the Grandstands

To gain more insight into the changes in community effected by the influence of the economic and media fields, I interviewed fourteen AFL and affiliate club members and fans of Australian football.[1] Even though the AFL and its clubs now market themselves to target consumers across all communities, regardless of their location or proximity, the majority of the football fans I interviewed support their clubs for reasons beyond money, marketing or the attractiveness of any club brand. From these individuals, we see confirmation of the commodification of play, the dominance of the economic field in the sport field, the influence of the media and the transformation of community. We also see their continuing passion for the sport, regardless of the changes that have occurred in the last thirty years and elements of genuine community alive at the grassroots level.

Becoming a fan

Few of the men and women interviewed have any recollection of consciously deciding to barrack for their teams. Most do so because of family relationships, friendships or proximity. Of those, family seems to be the strongest determinant of team affiliation, 'a family thing'.[2] Jason Lee concurs: 'My entire family barracks for Essendon…it's something that I've just always done.' Geelong supporter Neil Duncan attributes his team choice to his older brother: 'I was born in a country town, Yarrawonga, and he barracked for Geelong and he influenced a lot of things that I did at the time.'

Fathers influenced several of the interviewees. According to Scott Hutchins, 'Dad was a Geelong fan and I remember following them before I knew what they looked like, just because Dad was a Cats fan… I'm glad I did…[because] now that we're hours and hours apart, it's the one thing we regularly talk about.' Effie Caloutas 'barrack[s] for the NMFC because my father is an avid North Melbourne supporter'. Joshua Forte also identifies his father as the reason he supports Hawthorn: 'I was born in [the] 1986 premiership year…and my baby photos, I've got a [Hawthorn] beanie on.'

Grandparents were also influential. Alanna Ford remembers her grandmother, who was dying, bringing her 'up into her big double bed and [teaching her] the Carlton theme song – she was mad about the Blues, having grown up in Carlton. It's my only memory of her…but from that day forward there has been no doubt as to who my team is.' Kate Withers's grandfather encouraged her choice of the Geelong Cats: 'He would ferry my sisters and I down the highway to Kardinia Park for every home game.' With both her grandmother and her father barracking for South Melbourne, Cheree Brown says she 'was a Swans supporter as soon as I was born'; and Zak Kardachi has 'barracked for Essendon my whole life'.

For many fans, coming together to enjoy their common passion for AFL football strengthens family bonds. Scott Hutchins recalls the 2009 premiership and Paul Chapman kicking the 'winning goal in the last minute' of the game. He and his father 'both just jumped up and hugged'. According to Hutchins, 'That's probably the only time I've ever hugged my dad in my adult life.' Joshua Forte remembers sharing Hawthorn's win over Adelaide in the preliminary final: 'I got to share it with my brother, which was nice, just the two of us.' Although he didn't believe his brother was 'a sportsman or sport fan…when it comes to the Hawks… it was a close bond and you find yourself hugging each other'. He notes that this behaviour was typical of their younger days when 'growing up you might hate each other during the week, but when your family drives up to Waverley Park, it's common ground, you're barracking for the home club'. Jason Lee states that he 'spend[s] a lot of time talking to family and friends about footy', which 'ties into community'. According to Lee, 'You can be in a cab with a stranger you've never met and you ask them who they barrack for and straight away there's a connection.'

According to Huizinga, play stimulates traditions, which are often quite separate from ordinary and real life, which can be characterised by economic rationalist ideals.[3] Family, religious and sporting traditions and rituals are play-like phenomena that are not dictated by economic reasoning and therefore offer true insight into the culture of a community. So, although football clubs increasingly mirror businesses, which increasingly market and package themselves to attract new supporters and consumers of their brands, club loyalty may still be a matter of family tradition and the old-fashioned notion of barracking for the team that represents one's community.

However, not all of the interviewees barrack for their teams based on family traditions. Jeremiah Ryan attributes his choice of Collingwood to his three best friends: 'I barrack for the Pies because when I first went to primary school my three best friends all followed Collingwood', even though his mother and father each follow different teams (Sydney and North Melbourne respectively). Queenslander Tom Gallimore barracks for the team he believes represents his community: 'I've lived in Brisbane the majority of my life and that's been my team… They represent who I am, where I'm from and that's why I go for them.' He further explains that both he and his father feel a connection to the Brisbane Lions because they represent his home state: 'My father…[is] not a sport fan as such, but he appreciates sport and he barracks fiercely for Queensland and Brisbane teams… [H]e's proud that that's his state…and that's his city… I'm a lot more passionate about the Queensland perspective than a Brisbane perspective.'

Communicating with the club

Genuine community entails communication between the club and its members that allows members both to feel genuine ownership and the freedom to be their true selves and to work together towards achieving their club's shared and common goals. Unfortunately, based on the interviews, despite the use of the most up-to-date technology, communication between the AFL, its clubs and their members seems to be a monologue rather than a dialogue. They are not engaging members in ongoing conversation and are not inviting members to contribute collectively to assist the clubs in achieving their goals and objectives. Instead, the clubs engage in one-way communication, regardless of the number of channels they use or the technological savvy involved. The Swans use numerous communication channels to inform their members, according to Phil Wild: 'emails, Facebook updates, embedded videos and Twitter, all of which are 'that sort of stuff...[that] makes you feel part of it'. Even though Geelong uses social media to keep its members informed, Neil Duncan notes that the information is essentially 'just keeping you advised of each year to renew your membership [and] what functions are on'. On the other hand, Jason Lee feels that Essendon 'has become a lot better [at communicating] and very good at including you' and that 'the club has got better in engaging its supporters'. Kate Withers concurs, noting that Geelong is 'great at involving its supporters through social media...constantly inviting submissions for questions for press conferences'. Letting supporters get news related to the club 'before the traditional media outlets (television, newspapers and radio) can release the information' makes Effie Caloutas 'feel part of the community'.

Being part of the community

Genuine community involves citizens feeling that they belong, that they are part of the organisation, that they are coming together to enjoy something in common with other individuals. AFL clubs were originally structured to ensure that the controlling power of the club sits with its members, who elect the club's board of directors to represent them. It is their responsibility to act for and on behalf of, the members. In theory, the managers and administrators who make the day-to-day decisions are answerable to club members. Therefore, even though clubs may not be actively engaging their members in two-way conversation, members may still believe they have the ability to influence decisions and generate change within their clubs, that they can make a meaningful difference and that they are still the number one stakeholders in the AFL.

Most of the fans interviewed believe this is so. According to Neil Duncan, 'Ultimately, [the AFL] is still for the fans…but whether I agree with some of the decisions or sometimes it is influenced by forces outside the fan base…they are trying to keep it as mass appeal and that means making sure it appeals to the fans.' Scott Hutchins concluded that 'the fans are the number one stakeholder because without the fans, there's no game…no TV money…no betting money. It all dries up.'

Others, however, feel more detached from their clubs. Jeremiah Ryan notes that he is 'one of about 70,000 members. So I'm not going to always get a…personal sort of feeling from the club.' Michael Westland notes that there are 'different levels' of community within the clubs and that members who are part of the 'inner sanctum…feel a lot closer than I am'. The inner sanctum consists of the members who do, indeed, make genuine, active contributions to the club and engage with the club rather than around it. Scott Hutchins suggests that not growing up within the community also contributes to feelings of detachment: 'I've got a good mate who lives in Geelong, grew up there and I feel like he's very much part of the community, but having never lived in Geelong… I feel a bit out of it.' Alanna Ford explains that she doesn't feel as much a part of the club's community as she does a part of 'the community of supporters… I am instantly drawn and in love with other Carlton supporters.'

Making decisions

More important than statements of belief, however, are the recollections of times when these supporters stimulated change and directly influenced the decisions and actions of their clubs. Essendon member Michael Westland recalls that the club's decision to terminate the contract of its coach, Matthew Knights, was essentially due to the disenchantment of Essendon supporters and members because of the team's inconsistent performance under his leadership: 'The people voted with their feet…

and then the media got on board… so he was sacked… I'd like to think the supporter base let their feelings be known and that influenced, if not the final decision…the questions being asked in the first place.' Another Essendon member, Jason Lee, believes the club's decision to replace Knights with James Hird, a club legend with a huge supporter base, was also largely driven by the members: 'I think the hiring of James Hird as senior coach was a time when the members were listened to and the club made a decision based on a supporter base and what they would want… I think the club listened to the people on that one and employed [Hird].' For Phil Wild, the Sydney Swans' appointment of Paul Roos as coach in 2002 was a direct result of the club listening to its supporter base. The board had appointed Roos interim coach until the end of the season but was reportedly going to appoint the Western Bulldogs coach, Terry Wallace, to the position for the 2003 season. According to Wild, the strong support of the Sydney fans for Paul Roos changed the Sydney board's decision: 'The reputation he had with the club…blossomed… he's such a beloved member of the club and held in such high regard that… [the fans' views were] a factor.' Cheree Brown also recalled this particular decision: 'The Sydney fans overwhelming[ly] stood by Roos as "the people's choice", reviving the "Roooooos" calls at games. There was SO much support for Roos that eventually the club could not ignore it.'

However, most of the interviewees felt they had little input into decision making, which is 'nearly solely the realm of the board and its directors'. Although some felt that clubs still welcomed 'feedback and input', members had little impact on 'the bigger decisions', as Alanna Ford states, members and supporters have 'not one bit' of influence on decision making.

Conversely, interviewees could think of several club decisions that upset members and supporters. For Effie Caloutas, North Melbourne's 'letting Levi Greenwood go to Collingwood' was such a decision, although she notes that his lack of 'impact…due to an ankle injury has left some at ease with the decision'. Similarly, Swans supporters were unhappy with the club's decision to sign 'Buddy Franklin for a multimillion-dollar deal' but now seem content with the decision, even though the 'deal did result in…trade bans'.[4] The decision 'not to renew the contract of Paul Chapman' left 'every Geelong supporter…shattered', according to Kate Withers. In 2016 North Melbourne supporters felt the same about the sacking of Brent Harvey.

Citing a number of decisions Essendon made without member input, Stuart Osborne now believes that fans are no longer the club's number one stakeholders. Instead, more financially powerful stakeholders have become the club's primary custodians: 'If we were the number one stakeholder, then I think we would have input into the decisions of the club.' According to Osbourne, key decisions made without input from the Essendon membership include the relocation of the majority of home games from the Melbourne Cricket Ground to Etihad Stadium: 'When Essendon left the MCG it was a business decision basically… [T]hey basically made the recommendation to the members, put it to a vote and basically said we're going… So I don't think we are the number one stakeholder. I think there are other stakeholders that make the decisions.' Hawthorn supporter Josh Forte also believes that his club's decision to play four home games each year in Tasmania was based on financial gains rather than member input: 'I also see the enormous financial windfalls in doing that…[but] as a member, I think that's an enormous amount of games…which members miss out on.'

Although most interview participants acknowledge they rally together to generate desired outcomes for their clubs, they have also witnessed numerous occasions when the interest of the members is superseded by the need to generate revenue. Each club ultimately exists to win premierships, but each club can only exist if it is equipped with the necessary revenue streams to ensure its team can be competitive on the field. Because of the link between success on and off the field to off-field prosperity, clubs will always make decisions with the bottom line in mind, even if it means not seriously considering the needs and wishes of club members.

Participating financially

According to Stuart Osbourne, members are still important to football clubs but for financial reasons: 'We all sign up and pay memberships, so there's a financial input…[but] I think their [the members'] importance is more from an advocacy point of view because…we're all sort of like brand advocates of the brand that is [the] Essendon Football Club. I wear their gear and I go out and I talk about the company…every day, every week.' Many of the interviewees concur, viewing their financial contributions as active participation designed to help their clubs reach the shared goal of being successful on the field and ultimately of winning the premiership. Such is the dominance of economic capital within the sport field that fans and clubs alike see it as fundamentally necessary to the on-field success of their team.

For Jeremiah Ryan, being a member legitimates one's support of one's team: 'If you're a member…your money is where your mouth is. If you're a supporter, you're fly-by-night… [A] supporter is the sort of person who's not following the club when they're having…[a] bad run. A member, they've paid their money and they're always there.' Effie Caloutas has been a member of North Melbourne 'since the age of eight' because she 'love[s] the North Melbourne Football Club and…want[s] to help them in becoming a successful team'. Others, like Neil Duncan, did not join until their clubs begin experiencing financial distress: 'I joined when Geelong got into financial difficulty in the late 1980s and 90s and thought, well, I don't want to see them go into extinction, so I better do my little bit and join up as a member.'

Interviewees also feel that by buying memberships they are part of their clubs' communities. Kate Withers notes that 'the main reason' she is a member 'is to feel more a part of the club'. She feels she is 'investing both financially and emotionally in the club, which 'fills [her] with a sense of loyalty and belonging'. For Stuart Osbourne, purchasing a membership 'might be the only bit that I do every year…[but] it's about supporting the club…it's part of that whole experience of knowing that I'm one of 50,000 or 60,000 members'. Josh Forte concurs: 'Even if I buy a membership and I don't go to a game the whole year, I like to give back to an organisation or club that has given me so much joy and does give me so much joy.' According to Jason Lee, 'I'm a member because I just love the club. It's my greatest interest outside of family and work… I think (being a member) is a sense of contribution, you know, you feel like you're part of something if you're a member… [It] includes you in a group of people and I think you feel more part of it when you're a member.'

Other interviewees purchase memberships not to contribute to the achievement of a shared or common goal but to ensure their consumption of play as entertainment. A membership is essential for Zak Kardachi because it ensures he can attend games: 'If you want good seats, if you want to be at every game, then you buy a membership.' Rather than become a member of his football club, Michael Westland purchases memberships to both the Melbourne Cricket Club (MCC) and to the AFL: 'The MCC has the best rights…and [the] AFL membership' is basically to get grand final tickets. We've been to nearly every grand final ever since that I can remember.' So too does Geelong member Scott Hutchins, stating he buys a membership 'for me basically…it's mostly just for me'. Cheree Brown is 'an AFL member with Sydney Swans club support…because it gives [her] the option of deciding to go to the football to watch any game on the spur of the moment, without needing to book a ticket'. She also notes that she 'like[s] being guaranteed finals tickets…and attending special functions', although she also believes 'it's important to financially support your team'.

The interviewees' reasons for purchasing memberships reflect Thomas Frank's argument that community today is largely based on individual interests and that economic capital, which has become the foundation and building blocks of community, is at the core of freedom within a community.[5] Frank argues that this type of community is not real because it is based more on individualism than on the collective good. The majority of supporters I interviewed purchase memberships either for their personal benefit or for engaging with their club and feeling a part of its community. However, this engagement, this feeling of community, is based on financial contributions rather than on active involvement. The fact that club members feel they have to buy into their club communities to play a small role in helping their clubs achieve their ultimate goals supports Frank's assertions.

Coming together

Despite the changes within the AFL and its clubs, fans still seem to come together to enjoy the play element within the AFL. For many of the fans I interviewed, watching their teams play is a social experience. They watch with family or friends and often meet together either before or after matches to discuss the game they love. Footy outings involve her father, her sisters and friends and is 'never just attendance to the game', according to Kate Withers: 'It's a long public transport journey, followed by a pre-game meal and drinks, the game itself and then quite often more food and drinks' in addition to 'meet[ing] up with other friends at the game at half time.' Describing a typical outing, Josh Forte states that even though he receives a 'reserved seat' as a member of the club, he 'buy[s] a couple of MCC reserve tickets and we'll [Josh and his brother] go to the bar downstairs before the game... The first quarter is just me and my brother...and then it's a catch up with some friends, watch a bit of football, then talk with others... So it's a big social opportunity.'

For Jason Lee, the match is 'a good place to catch up with people, family or friends. It is very much a social thing.' Tom Gallimore states that he prefer[s] to be watching with mates...[to] hang out with someone that I enjoy hanging out with and watching the game that I enjoy watching... it does connect us'. For Neil Duncan, the experience is social: 'I like meeting people. I like interacting with people and I love [watching] the game live as it is a much better experience than watching it on television... it's the whole social fabric around it, you have a drink and you have a chat, Monday morning you can't wait to talk about it.' Although she enjoys games with friends and family, Cheree Brown also likes to attend by herself: 'I can put my headphones in, listen to the commentary and really concentrate on the game.' When she does go with other people, they often get together before the game 'for a quick drink' and after the game 'go out for a drink or dinner somewhere close to the ground'.

Thus, the AFL does still stimulate people to come together to enjoy something in common with others and to socialise before and after the game, actively engaging in conversation about the game. This certainly mirrors the activity that once occurred within the clubrooms of the VFL/AFL and which still occurs within local, grassroots community clubs. However, what once occurred within the club now occurs outside the club, often in pubs, bars and restaurants. This social interaction between fans is also fundamentally based on a shared enjoyment in consuming AFL football, not on a common sense of loyalty, obligation or responsibility to work together to help their clubs achieve their shared goals.

Instead, according to Baudrillard, the social interaction and experience of football fans appears to be a simulation of community.[6] That is not to say that the social interaction between fans is pointless or in complete opposition to community. On the contrary, coming together to enjoy something in common with others is at the heart of what defines community. However, because fans are now just one of many important financial stakeholders, they are less engaged in the decision-making process of their clubs and seem increasingly less engaged in actively working within their clubs to help them reach their common or shared goal of on-field success. Therefore, although consuming play in the AFL creates and maintains social bonds and social interactions, it neither creates nor sustains the community that Huizinga describes.

As the AFL and its clubs continue to evolve into businesses, the relationships between the league, its clubs and their members evolve. Today the AFL and its clubs are top-down organisations that appear to stand quite separately from their supporters. What community exists within each club is formed in a fundamentally different manner from the communities created at the founding of the game. Becoming part of a football club's community and participating actively within that community now consist of purchasing a membership to support the club financially, which fans perceive as a legitimate means to help their club succeed and advance toward the ultimate goal of winning a premiership.

10

A Global Phenomenon

Unfortunately, the merger of the sport field with the economic and media fields and the subsequent transformation of play into display are not unique to the AFL. Rather, the AFL is but one example of what is undoubtedly a world trend in a global and media era. Some may even argue that compared with other professional sporting leagues, such as the English Premier League (EPL), the influence of money in the AFL is rather modest. Regardless of whether that is true or not, looking at the transformation in another sport, the 'world game' of soccer, may help us understand where the AFL may be headed and what may be in store for the AFL community as the game they once built and owned continues to evolve and transform into a business.

Without question, soccer at the elite level of competition is one of the most commercialised and commodified games in world sport. Most of its premier leagues and the clubs in the sport's various elite competitions function as businesses. Indeed, many of the clubs in the EPL are privately owned entities with some even listed on the stock exchange. They trade in play and spend millions of dollars on ensuring success both on and off the field. In soccer, money appears to be at the heart of the game.

The players

Individual players in world soccer earn significantly more than their AFL counterparts. Players in the premier leagues in Europe are paid enormous amounts of money per match to represent their clubs. Unlike the AFL, the governing bodies of these leagues do not impose salary caps on the total player payments of any league team. Richer clubs often find themselves in bidding wars for the best players, with the winners usually the clubs who can offer players the most money. Thus, the richest clubs in the world, such as Manchester United, Manchester City, FC Bayern Munich, Chelsea, FC Barcelona, Real Madrid, Juventus and Inter Milan, attract the most elite players to their clubs. These clubs can also invest in the best training equipment, recovery methods and sport science to ensure the players on their lists are more skilful, better prepared and ultimately more successful than players on the other teams. Unsurprisingly, the teams that finish higher on the ladder in these soccer competitions also happen to be among the wealthiest.

The extreme influence of economic capital in professional soccer reached excessive levels in 2007 when David Beckham signed a contract to play for the Los Angeles Galaxy for $175,000 a day for five years. This equals $1.2 million per week and $320 million over the life of the contract (including salary and endorsements). However, this trend was not new. In Spain, the rich and resource-wealthy club Real Madrid had bought a host of players in the early 2000s: Figo in 2000, Zidane in 2002 and Beckham in 2003, for a combined total of up to €2000 million.[1] In 2015, Real Madrid's Cristiano Ronaldo was the world's highest paid footballer, earning €79 million for the year, which included both his player salary and endorsement deals. Barcelona's Lionel Messi earned €70.5 million for the year, followed by Zlatan Ibrahimovic of Paris Saint-Germain FC (€41.8 million) and Real Madrid's Gareth Bale (€34.9 million).[2]

Although the monies proffered are extreme, the richest players in professional soccer do not just play for pay. The relationships they share with their clubs are based on million-dollar contracts that make them some of the wealthiest people not just in the sport and entertainment fields but in society, leading also to their individual sponsorship deals. Their contracts represent not just money but also power, prestige and celebrity status. Thus, imagining players turning down contracts giving them increases in the millions of dollars to stay with their current clubs and to uphold the notions of loyalty and community is difficult.

The play element

The influence of economic capital has also transformed the play element in soccer to a far greater extent than in the AFL. In soccer, play is now a commodity utilised by both players and clubs to generate success on the field and profitability. Clubs in the world's strongest and richest soccer leagues trade players and lend, lease and borrow players to make money, save money or simply win games. Thus, the connection a player has to a club appears subordinate to winning and making money.

Because clubs can trade players during either of two transfer periods in the calendar year, one between seasons and one within the season, players may begin the season with one club but end it with another club. Clubs can also loan or lease their players to rival clubs throughout the season to save money or to help players develop without having to play them on their own teams. For example, an EPL club such as Manchester United may lend a player to Queens Park Rangers (QPR) for a specified number of games throughout the season. The borrowing club (QPR) pays a percentage (often 100 per cent) of the player's wages to use the player during those games. The loaning club (Manchester United) saves money on player wages and also receives the added bonus of ensuring the player is getting match practice and development in playing for the borrowing club.[3] Such arrangements generally occur between richer clubs and poorer clubs.

In *A Beautiful Game? Searching for the Soul of Football*, David Conn describes the use of these practices by two English football clubs, Leeds and Bradford. These clubs sold players to a hire-purchase company based in Guernsey and then leased them back to save money and, thus, increase their profit margins. The hire-purchase company utilised the players as ambassadors to advocate and sell their service, which clubs recognised as an opportunity to increase their profits.[4] Such practices confirm the transformation of the play element into a business practice, a tool to make or save money. Players are commodities, representing the club for whom they are playing in any given match. They play because they are contracted to do so, which is quite different from playing for love or passion for the community, the club or the game, without pay.

Trading, borrowing, lending and leasing are distinctly different in the AFL. Apart from a period between 1990 and 1993 when the AFL implemented a trial mid-year draft, trading occurs between seasons only. Thus, players remain with the same team for the entire season and cannot play for any other team during the season.[5] AFL rules also stipulate players cannot be leased, loaned or borrowed during the season. Such practices are ultimately based on gaining some kind of economic advantage; but because of the AFL-imposed salary cap, they cannot generate the same benefit in the AFL that they do in world soccer. The salary cap serves to ensure not only a certain sense of evenness, equality and egalitarianism in the AFL but also the retention of some sense of community spirit and loyalty as part of the defining characteristics of the play element in the AFL. Thus, because AFL players are paid very modestly in comparison with elite soccer players, other aspects of playing carry greater significance, including loyalty to one's club and teammates.

The World Cup, held every four years, also reveals the link between wealth and play that defines the play element on the field. Teams and players represent countries from most continents of the world. Although these nations are equally passionate in striving for the world championship, the stark differences in equipment, infrastructure and resources between rich and poor nations result in poorer nations having to battle to succeed and win on the field.

The media

The influence of the media field in the sport field has distanced the game from the community while heightening the transformation of play into display. When BSkyB, a pay television network, won the rights to broadcast all games in the EPL in 1992, fans had to pay a subscription fee to watch their teams play.[6] On 10 February 2015, Sky and BT pay television networks purchased the exclusive rights to broadcast all matches played in the EPL from 2016 to 2019 for £5.1 billion, effectively eliminating the ability of supporters to watch their teams play for free. BSkyB and BT's exclusive ownership of broadcast rights to all EPL games is a stark example of the play element in English soccer being taken away from grassroots supporters of the game and sold back to the them in the form of entertainment to ensure television broadcasters can profit. These networks treat supporters of the game as consumers, effectively forcing them to buy the right to consume play as entertainment.

This is distinctly different from television broadcasting rights in the AFL. Although both pay and free-to-air networks package games to appeal to the hearts and minds of Australian consumers, fans may choose whether to pay or not, depending on how many games they wish to see. Currently, four games each week of the AFL home and away season are shown on free-to-air television, ensuring grassroots football fans can watch their teams play. Fans also have the option of subscribing to Foxtel, a pay television network, which owns the rights to broadcast all nine games live. These choices give football fans the option of either paying for the right to watch all games live or watching a limited number of games each week for free. Thus, even though pay broadcasts are a significant transformation of play in the AFL, they are still well short of what has occurred in English soccer.

Community

More than any other game, soccer has the rare ability to bring diverse people together to enjoy and appreciate something in common with others. The World Cup is an excellent example of this ability. From across the globe, men and women of various cultures, backgrounds, religions and political persuasions sit together in the grandstands to enjoy these games. Yet even this celebration of togetherness exhibits the influence of economic capital and the unity just described is more momentary than lasting.[7] Where sporting clubs and teams were once the hub of social and community activity, defined by a common grassroots appreciation for the club, the players or the community from which they spawned, teams in the World Cup are so professional and elite that they are 'out of reach'. Thus, soccer fans at the World Cup unite with their friends and fellow compatriots in the grandstands, without having any personal connection to the players or the teams beyond nationalistic attachment. While invoking a sense of national pride and belonging, these are hardly conditions for the generation of community.

Ramifications for the AFL

Comparatively, the AFL and world soccer are not at the same levels of commodification. The effects of the merger of the economic, media and sport fields are much more pronounced in soccer and quite possibly in other world sport as well. Nevertheless, Australian football as played in the AFL is steadily progressing toward the same levels and, with every step forward, becomes less and less the people's game.

The ramifications of the continued commodification of the play element in the AFL and the increasing influence of the economic and media fields are several. Among them is the deterioration of community as it was at the game's founding and in the early days of the VFL and as it still is to some extent in local grassroots clubs throughout Australia. Yet, despite its transformation and its embracing of neoliberal principles, the AFL still exhibits some of the characteristics present in the beginning of the people's game. To stem the tide of increasing commodification and the resulting destabilization of community, then, we must understand where the AFL currently stands.

11

The AFL Today

Sport is now a business, consumed by spectators and discussed every day of the week in newspapers and magazines; on television and radio; in boardrooms, offices and homes; in pubs and lounge rooms; and online on websites, blogs and Facebook pages. The Australian Football League is the epitome of this transformation. Since its redesignation in 1990, the AFL has expanded its franchise, found new markets, attracted new fans and supporters and increased its revenue streams dramatically. It now reaches all the states and territories of the nation and mirrors the capitalist and bureaucratic business model of Western civilisation. What started as people gathering to enjoy the game of Australian football together as a community has morphed into a multibillion-dollar industry.

Attendance

The popularity of the AFL continues to grow. In 2015, the eighteen competing clubs in the AFL participated in 207 games at sixteen venues, representing each state and territory in Australia, over the twenty-three weeks of the Toyota AFL Premiership season. During the premiership season, 6,351,578 Australians attended AFL games. With an average crowd size of 32,242 people per game, the AFL had the fourth highest average crowd attendance of all professional sports in the world. Only the USA's National Football League (68,278), Germany's Bundesliga Football League (43,527) and the English Premier League (36,175) attracted bigger crowds.[1] The average Australian television audience each week was 4.466 million. Another 1.152 million listened to the matches on radio.

Following the premiership season were the four weeks of the Toyota AFL finals series, including eight finals and the grand final. A total of 3.534 million Australians watched the AFL grand final at home on television.[2]

Venues

Gone are the traditional suburban grounds, with their folksy names that characterised their locations and quirky characteristics: Windy Hill, the Western Oval, the Junction Oval, Moorabbin, Princess Park, Punt Road Oval, Victoria Park, Glenferrie Oval and Arden Street Oval. Some of these have become training venues for their multimillion dollar clubs and players; others have ceased to serve even in that capacity.

In their place are venues that reflect the influence of the economic field and the clubs' needs for economic capital. These venues carry the names of corporate sponsors, who have paid millions of dollars for the right to name their clubs' grounds and stadiums: Etihad Stadium (at first branded as Colonial Stadium and then Telstra Stadium), AAMI Stadium, ANZ Stadium, Domain Stadium and Simonds Stadium.

Team structure

The structure of each club is based on a business format. Each of the eighteen AFL clubs is governed by a board of directors charged with structuring the club to ensure its financial viability. Although each club may be slightly different in its hierarchical structure, each board employs a chief executive officer and relevant department managers to operate the organisation as a business. Because the goal of these boards is to generate success both on and off the field, they are now commonly composed of businessmen, such as Collingwood's Alex Waislitz, a millionaire businessman and friend of club president and media personality Eddie McGuire.[3]

Collingwood is arguably the AFL's biggest club, with more than 75,000 members and an average home-and-away crowd of 47,259.[4] In

2011, Collingwood won twenty games over twenty-two rounds of the AFL home and away season before losing the grand final to Geelong. The club posted total revenue earnings of $75,592,030, with a profit of $2,141,436.[5] According to Waislitz, Collingwood's success on and off the field is largely due to its being governed and operated as a business: 'You can't afford not to be a business as the cost of fielding a football team is enormous – between $9 million and $12 million a year.'[6] Collingwood member Jeremiah Ryan supports this view of the division of labour between the president of the club, Eddie McGuire and the coach, Nathan Buckley: 'They've each got their own department that they look after and they look after them well… [W]hether it's the Collingwood Football Club or the St Michael's Football Club…or the Swinburne Football Club… the president takes care of business, the coach coaches the team and the captain represents the players.'

Over the last few decades, other clubs have also turned to high-flying businessmen and women to preside over operations, such as John Elliott (Carlton), Christopher Skase (Brisbane Bears), Geoffrey Edelsten (Sydney Swans), Joseph Gutnick (Melbourne), David Smorgon (Western Bulldogs), Paul Gardiner (Melbourne), Frank Costa (Geelong), Jeff Kennett (Hawthorn), Richard Pratt (Carlton), David Evans (Essendon), Paul Little (Essendon) and Andrew Newbold (Hawthorn). This reflects a major shift from the ex-players and influential community supporters who dominated club governance until the late 1990s. Geelong member Neil Duncan notes the importance of a stable club management structure for sustained on-field success: 'Frank Costa (former president), Brian Cook (chief executive officer) and "Bomber" Thompson (former coach)…are probably the three people I think of because they took us from debt, millions of dollars in debt and a club that was really a rabble – our captain had walked out…and now three premierships later, (we have) a new ground that is now going to hold close to 40,000 (spectators) with lights they were the three people who took the club from nowhere to where it is.' According to Duncan, the president, CEO and coach have taken the Geelong Football Club 'from a broke club that didn't look like playing finals to a club that is profitable, admired and…a thriving business that is developing, increasing membership, a new ground with lights and threatening to at least make finals and win premierships most years.'

The AFL's 2015 annual report revealed total revenue of $494.1 million, an increase of 7 per cent. The report also showed a record operating surplus of $337.8 million, a net profit of $2.5 million and accumulated net assets valued at $125.973 million.[7] These figures indicate the AFL is undeniably a business and simulates the bureaucratic business model that dominates the Western world. Play is a commodity and a product within the sporting industry and, more broadly, within the entertainment industry. As Andrew Demetriou, former AFL chief executive officer, pointed out in his 2005 annual report, the AFL is not only a brand and a business but also a form of entertainment that must compete with all other forms of entertainment for the attention, interest and loyalty of the Australian people.[8]

Stuart Osbourne highlights this transformation in his reflections of the Essendon Football Club:

> In the 1980s they (players) were going to training two nights a week and playing a game on Saturday and going out for a few cans after the game. So, basically (now) you've got full time footballers and full time departments. I mean ten years ago, there weren't even football departments. You had a coach and a few runners or trainers or whatever and a doctor, of course. But these days, it's just a function of the professionals…which comes back to the money that's come into the game players are (now) full time and they're surrounded by full time support staff because there's so much money in the game.

Media

In 1998, 621 accredited journalists and broadcasters covered the AFL. By 2013, this figure had almost doubled to 1,073.[9] Coverage of the game, both on and off field occurs 365 days a year, as an unquenchably thirsty media broadcasts the AFL and its clubs to every corner of the nation. As Brian Walsh, former head of corporate affairs and communications for the AFL, stated in the 2010 annual report, 'The coverage of Australian Football has moved from a seasonal pursuit to 24/7, 365 day a year coverage where the growth in traditional media coverage has been matched or exceeded by the growth in online coverage.'[10]

The major metropolitan newspapers, particularly in the AFL stronghold states of Victoria, Tasmania, South Australia and Western Australia, have learned that the AFL sells papers, regardless of the time of year. Newspapers such as the *Herald Sun*, the number-one-selling paper in Australia, provide extensive coverage of the AFL and its games all year round. For example, on Friday, 9 December 2011, deep into the AFL's off season, the *Herald Sun* contained nine AFL-related stories spread over six pages of the sport section, outweighing the coverage of all other sport.[11] During the football season, papers often include sport supplements of AFL-related stories, with columnists and so-called football experts generating conversation about the game and its issues. These supplements are often up to twenty pages in length. AFL stories are also sensationally splashed across the front pages of the daily newspapers to increase sales. Football and its players sell newspapers even in the summer months of the AFL's off season. Such extensive coverage, once limited to the actual AFL football season and to reports about on-field results and players' performance, reflects the ability of the AFL's popularity to sell papers.

Many radio stations also cover the AFL extensively and have incorporated the game as an integral part of their scheduling. Throughout the AFL season, radio stations 3AW, the ABC, Triple M, SEN, K Rock, 6PR, 5AA, the National Indigenous Radio Services Network and AFL Live (Crocmedia) combine to broadcast all AFL games of the home and away season and finals, reaching over one million people each week.[12] These radio stations have built many magazine-style sport programs into their scheduling, especially during the high-rating drive-time slots, to attract listeners. Programs such as *Sport Today* on Melbourne's 3AW and *The Rush Hour* on Melbourne's Triple M are sport-based programs hosted by ex-AFL players and personalities. Program content is anchored extensively in AFL football, including both the on-field performance of players and teams and off-field issues about players, AFL personalities and clubs. During the AFL season, football constitutes most of the content for these programs.

In 2004, Melbourne's Sport Entertainment Network (SEN) became the second radio station (behind the Racing and Sport Network, previously Sport 927) dedicated wholly and completely to sport and targeted at sport enthusiasts. Most of the program hosts are either ex-AFL football players or current AFL commentators. Most of the content involves discussions about the AFL, its players, clubs and teams and on- and off-field issues about the game.

However, television has undoubtedly had the greatest impact and influence on the play element in the AFL. In 2015, the AFL sold the television broadcasting rights to all AFL pre-season, home and away and finals series games to the Seven Network and Foxtel for a record $2.508 billion.[13] As part of the deal, Seven broadcast three games each weekend of the AFL season on Friday night, Saturday night and Sunday afternoon. The network also broadcast an additional eleven games live across the season. These games included five or six Thursday night games and games played on the eve of public holidays and on public holidays. Foxtel broadcast all nine AFL games each week of the AFL home and away season on their AFL-dedicated Fox Footy station. The network also hosts AFL-specific magazine-style programs, including *AFL Teams*, *On the Couch*, *AFL 360* and *After the Bounce*.

Australian free-to-air stations have embraced the AFL as a ratings winner and means of generating large audiences for waiting advertisers. Throughout the 2016 season, AFL-specific magazine-style programs centred on play in the AFL, with issues around the game comprising a relatively large portion of each network's program scheduling. These programs included Seven's *Game Day* and *Talking Footy*; ABC's *Offsiders*; and Nine Network's *Sunday Football Show*, *Footy Classified* and *The Footy Show*, which entered its twenty-third season in 2016.

This increased influence of the media field, which reflects the play–money–media cycle, has not gone unnoticed by supporters and fans. In discussing the effects of the media on the game, Jason Lee notes coverage 'is now twenty-four hours; it's on multiple television channels, every radio station, newspapers, front and back'. Jeremiah Ryan concurs: 'Where I work we've got Fox Footy. That's a whole channel. All it does is talk about footy. That wasn't there thirty years ago. It just wasn't.' Scott Hutchins has also noticed the saturation: 'When I was a kid…the *Footy Show* was the only dedicated football show outside the football coverage itself, whereas now we've got Fox Footy – there's Gerard Whately and Mark Robinson giving their thoughts on the game every night of the week.' According to Michael Westland, the media has influenced his consumption of the game: 'I remember football growing up as Friday night, Saturday night, Sunday…every Saturday afternoon was consumed by local football… But these days footy is all encompassing. I'm a huge fan of Fox Footy and I can plan my night purely based around Fox Footy.'

In commenting on the impact of the media, Effie Caloutas believes the media have 'exposed the game to the public…increas[ing] participation through the grassroots and enhanc[ing] its popularity'. On the other hand, Stuart Osbourne suggests that media coverage of actual games has superseded the interests of football fans: 'There are too many bloody timeslots. And I know it's all done for TV so that every game can be shown live, but it's frigging impossible to plan your weekend when you go to the footy now. It's like there's a 1.10 p.m. game, a 1.40 p.m. game, there's a 2.10 p.m. game, there's a 4.10 p.m. game, there's a 7.10 p.m., a 7.40 p.m. – and it's all driven by broadcasters because they want every game live.'

Still, Osbourne avidly consumes media sources for information on football, as do many of the supporters I interviewed:

> I check *The Age* website on my phone… I'll have to go through the general news to get down to [the] sport [section]… And the AFL app – in terms of my media consumption, it would be one of my more frequent apps, especially on the weekends – not just for Essendon games, but for other games too and then obviously SEN in terms of the radio. So my media consumption is almost, I'd say, 100 per cent [football] because I listen to SEN and it's really all they talk about. In terms of my phone, most of it would be footy and then TV is about the only more balanced thing.

Jeremiah Ryan also relies on apps to stay informed: 'I've got the AFL app on my iPad and I use that for scores when I'm at work or when I'm travelling…and I can watch a replay of Collingwood when I'm at work if I missed it.' Caloutas and Brown also referred to staying abreast of footy news through social media.

According to Scott Hutchins, '90 per cent plus' of his media consumption is related to sport:

> Really just basically Friday night…through to Sunday 7 o'clock, when the twilight game finishes. I would usually probably average attending one game a week and I'd probably watch three to four games on TV. If I couldn't watch my TV, I'd listen to the [game] they've got on the radio if I had access to it. And if I didn't have access to any of that, I would be checking the scores on my phone.

Josh Forte's media consumption of the AFL is also substantial, although somewhat less than that of other interviewees: 'I'd say 50 per cent… I will read just about any article that will come up during the day. I just like to be across it, but I regard AFL [to be] in that news frame because it's something that impacts me. It's big business.'

Interestingly, Michael Westland describes his involvement with football through the media as 'embarrassing':

> I surround myself with it…if I open the *Herald Sun* (on the internet)…I open probably twelve windows of articles I want to read, half will be football… When I go to work in the morning, I listen to Triple M [with] Eddie McGuire, Luke Darcy and Mick Molloy, of which 80 per cent of the conversation is about football. On the way home from work, I listen to James Brayshaw and Billy Brownless, who are consumed nearly wholly with football. And when I'm at work, I often listen to SEN, which is again consumed nearly wholly by football. And it's purely, it's entertaining… I find it informative and entertaining. And I love it.

The interviewees also commented on some of the changes in coverage ultimately resulting from the merger of the economic, media and sport fields. Jason Lee, for example, notes that 'footballers have now become celebrities, not sport people' and that anyone connected with the club has come under intense 'scrutiny': 'With the advent of social media –

you know, Twitter, Facebook – an incident simultaneously just goes viral into the community... The media has had a massive change and it's certainly had a huge impact on the way the game's seen.' Cheree Brown concurs, noting that such scrutiny of 'footballers and coaches...can affect their performance'. The mushrooming media coverage has caused Zak Kardachi to speculate, 'What do you write about as a news outlet when the news only happens two days a week?... [Y]ou have to fill seven days-worth of news and I think that's added a lot of sensationalism, a lot of off-field talk that perhaps wasn't there before... [T]en to fifteen years ago who would've known who the CEO of the club was and who would've cared if they resigned?' Jason Lee concurs, indicating this is 'a new phenomenon': 'I know probably by name four or five people on the Essendon board. If you asked me that ten or fifteen years ago, I would have no idea... [T]he level of information is far more readily available on what's happening at a club. The media's had a massive role to play in that.'

For Alanna Ford, however, the impact of media has been far from favourable, noting that the decreasing number of games available on free-to-air television is making it 'hard for some people trying to get their kids to get wrapped up in the wonder of footy'. She states that in some families she knows the 'kids are no longer interested in footy because of lack of access to their team's games'. As a result, they 'now follow soccer or basketball'. Ford also laments the stultification nature of media scrutiny, which has caused 'players and coaching staff [to] all speak from the same media training handbook. It is very rare that you get a player, especially, speaking authentically. You can almost hear the media manager waving their hands violently in the background saying, "No, cut the comment!"' Thus, fans and supporters are cognisant of the influence the media has over the AFL and on the decisions that affect Australian football. As Kate Withers states, 'Clubs and the AFL itself are now beholden to the demands of advertisers, sponsors and broadcast partners... The game itself wouldn't exist without investment from media outlets, so advertising needs have taken priority over the actual integrity and purity of the game itself.' Phil Wild concurs: 'I think you'd be a bit naïve not to think that [the media has the biggest say in decisions]. While generally what the media want and what the fans want would hopefully be sort of congruent [where] we're pushing in the same direction, when push comes to shove... I mean, money talks, unfortunately.'

Revenue

The media's strong influence has exacerbated commercialisation and commodification of the AFL brand. Regardless of whether or not the AFL's need and desire for money is a cause or a consequence of the play–money–media cycle, the AFL no longer seeks capital autonomous to other fields. Instead, it actively pursues economic capital and media exposure to the point of assisting with packaging the game as entertainment to attract consumers.

The influence of economic capital in the AFL extends to the way the game is viewed, measured and discussed. In this context, the conversation about the game mirrors conversation about business to such an extent that it simulates the language used when discussing the market. As part of the AFL 2015 annual report, the AFL measured its performance in the same ways business does, using its key financial indicators to measure the success of the competition:

- Revenue was $494.1 million, an increase of 7 per cent.
- The operating surplus was $337.8 million, an increase of $19.7 million.
- The net profit equalled $2.5 million.
- Total operating expenditures were $156.3 million, an increase of 10 per cent.
- Distributions to clubs increased to $335.2 million

Furthermore, after AFL distributions, eight of the league's eighteen clubs recorded a profit in 2015.[14]

The AFL's net profit of $2.5 million is a relatively small number compared with other professional sporting competitions around the world. This is largely due to the AFL putting most of its revenue back into the game in the form of distributions to its eighteen clubs. Such distributions highlight the importance of television broadcasting rights to the AFL. Because several clubs have had trouble transforming into commercial brands and businesses, the $2.508 billion generated from these rights allow many of the clubs to survive. These revenues also reflect the power of the media and the resulting reliance the AFL has on the media to ensure their competition remains a vibrant industry and an exciting entertainment product for Australian consumers.

Supporters of AFL teams have also acknowledged the AFL's transformation into a business. According to Sydney Swans member Phil Wild,

> At its heart, it's a business. It might be…a not-for-profit business, in that its business aims are not the same as a typical corporation. It obviously doesn't aim to make money, its aim is basically to promote the game of AFL, benefit the players, benefit the supporters, but it still has to be run like a business because its main competitors are other sport. If you don't react to the marketplace and try to take steps to protect your position then you're going to get found out.

Essendon supporter Jason Lee describes the AFL as 'obviously a national competition, professional and organised; it's a business, you know, it's a multibillion-dollar organisation now and it's glamorous'.

Thus, the AFL is undeniably a business within the entertainment industry. At the heart of its operation is both the need and desire for economic capital, exacerbated by the play–money–media cycle. The resulting play element in the AFL today is neither what it was at its founding nor what Huizinga argues it should be:[15]

- It is no longer free.
- It is no longer separate from ordinary or real life.
- It is no longer without serious outcomes limited only to the field of play.
- It is no longer a grassroots item of folk culture, stimulated by communal passion, spirit and action.

Instead, the economic and media fields have imposed upon the play element, selling it to consumers as entertainment. Thus, the AFL serves as an example of the consequences for the community and culture when the sport field merges with the economic and media fields.

12

Re-establishing Community

As we have seen, Australian football as played in the AFL is no longer a game primarily derived from the passions of the citizens that play it; nor does it engender community within those citizens. In merging with the economic and media fields, the sport field has become a multi-billion-dollar business within the entertainment industry. Neoliberal ideals and principles dominate participants' decisions and actions on the field in the endless pursuit of economic capital and an increasingly intense drive to generate profits. This desire for money has compromised the spontaneity, flair, creativity and freedom of play in the AFL. In their place are carefully managed game plans, set plays, tactics, structures and detailed microanalyses to ensure victory.

As a result, Australian football no longer has the ability to stimulate genuine communities. The ongoing struggle for economic capital has largely replaced the old-fashioned notions of loyalty, tradition, ritual and the active participation of the community within the football club. Key stakeholders no longer include members, supporters and the community at large but those whose decisions affect the financial growth and stability of the clubs. The new number one stakeholders use the bottom line as their guide in making any and all decisions affecting the AFL and its eighteen clubs.

Exacerbating the drive for economic capital are the media, reflected in the play–money–media cycle, which is at the heart of the AFL's existence. The increased revenue generated from unprecedented television broadcasting rights deals implemented over the last decade has not only provided an enormous injection of money into the AFL but also accelerated the transformation of the AFL and its play element begun over thirty years ago. The media utilise the AFL as a tool to attract large audiences. The larger the audience, the more revenue the media can generate from advertisers. Radio and television broadcasters can also promote programming during AFL matches, increasing not only audiences but also the advertising revenues from those programs. The AFL assists by packaging, marketing, promoting and selling itself to consumers as entertainment, transforming the game into a show starring the football players. In return, the AFL generates the revenue needed to survive and thrive in the ever competitive entertainment industry.

The media have become the driver for decision making in both the AFL and each of its clubs. Play is now serious and is no longer separate from the ordinary and real. Players serve as commodities utilised by the AFL, their clubs and the media as tools to promote and sell the game. They no longer participate strictly for fun, fitness or enjoyment. Instead, playing football is now their job. As such, today's AFL players receive more compensation than any group before them. Thus, money, not loyalty and community, is increasingly at the heart of players' relationships with their clubs.

To ensure the generation of sufficient revenue to survive, the AFL and its clubs are now structured as businesses, complete with football departments, various levels of management and boards of directors whose primary objective is not only to win games but also to remain financially viable. Both players and the play element are their primary assets. Thus, winning is reduced to a function of business that subverts the spontaneity, creativity, flair and enjoyment of playing into micromanaged play to ensure teams perform in the most efficient and effective manner possible. Indeed, the influence of highly paid coaches, managers and sport scientists has threatened the integrity of the game.

The overall business strategy of the AFL for the past thirty years has seemingly been to evolve into a national product with a national television audience to attract increasing amounts of revenue from the sale of broadcast rights. The relocation of South Melbourne to Sydney, Fitzroy's merger with Brisbane, the addition of the Gold Coast Suns and the Greater Western Sydney Giants and the rejection of Tasmania's bid for an AFL team all illustrate the influence of the media in determining the strategic direction of the AFL since the late 1970s.

Just as players have become commodities, so have AFL members and supporters become revenue sources, subverted by the powers of economic capital. No longer are they the hearts and souls of their clubs, a genuine part of their communities involved in enriching and contributing to life within their clubs and working toward common goals. The South Melbourne Football Club could not stop its relocation to Sydney. The Fitzroy community could not stop its merger and subsequent relocation. The community uprising and passion of the Tasmanians could not sway the AFL to grant them a franchise. Thus, unlike the oldest VFL clubs built by the people for the people as an expression of their shared passion for the game, the AFL manufactured and sold its newest franchises to new consumers as attractive items of entertainment.

The fans and supporters interviewed as part of this research are exceedingly aware of the AFL's transformation into a business and of the increasing influence of money and the media within the AFL. They acknowledge the growing influence of coaches and management at each club; the use of more set plays, game plans and structures; and the giving of more instructions for players to follow than ever before. All of these, they note, have reduced the creativity and inventiveness of players.

Of greater importance, however, are the interviewees' descriptions of their interaction with the AFL and its clubs, which reflect the inability of these clubs to stimulate genuine community. As Huizinga argues, genuine community results from citizens

- coming together in an autonomous setting to enjoy something in common with others;
- feeling a sense of belonging and meaning;
- forming strong emotional ties with other members of the community;
- feeling a sense of loyalty, obligation or responsibility to each other; and

- influencing and actively contributing to the common shared goals of the community.[1]

Although AFL football is still a platform to come together to enjoy something in common with others, citizens do so outside the football clubs. Instead of meeting together within the confines of their clubs, they meet at pubs, restaurants or cafés for drinks or meals or within the stadiums. When asked if they feel part of their club's community, the interviewees could only cite occasions when the game evoked emotional ties with fellow supporters. Outside of purchasing club memberships and barracking in the grandstands, these individuals revealed few, if any, active contributions to their clubs. Instead, they apparently see their financial contributions as actively engaging with and contributing to, their club, actions that also evidence the AFL's use of supporters as sources of revenue.

Despite promoting its clubs to their members via social and digital media channels, the AFL does not invite them to contribute actively to their clubs. Members are no longer empowered to make decisions as each club now has a manager to make decisions about the club's future. This business structure removes members from active engagement and treats them as consumers rather than as owners. They no longer feel free to act within their clubs' communities and, as such, can participate only in restricted and passive ways. Thus, they feel alienated from the clubs that were once communities.

This contrasts sharply with interviewees' reflections on their involvement with local grassroots clubs. These fans feel they are genuinely part of these clubs and actively participate in them. Thus, although the AFL and its clubs create some sense of community, its ability to stimulate the sense of belonging, freedom, empowerment, active engagement and sense of obligation and responsibility to fellow members that engender feelings of satisfaction and self-worth from enriching the community appears limited.

We must understand, however, that the AFL and its play element are still transforming. A comparison to other professional and commercialised sporting organisations around the world clearly shows that the AFL has maintained a relative sense of egalitarianism, accessibility, fairness and equality – all characteristics of the democratic values upon which Australia was founded. Indeed, the AFL and its clubs are active within the community, its players are still relatively modestly paid, the cost to attend matches live is still relatively affordable and citizens can still avail themselves of free television and radio broadcasts. However, the stark capitalist, neoliberal, economically rationalist characteristics of other sporting organisations are clear warnings of the direction in which the AFL may be headed as transformation continues.

Over the last three decades, professional sport has lost its autonomy, its separation from the market economy. The more it is influenced by money, the more the play element has been transformed and the relationship between the fans and the game has been weakened. This, in turn, has weakened communities, thus affecting the ability of individuals to reach their full potential and undermining the democratic ideals on which Australia was founded.

Trend reversal

To turn this trend or at least slow it, we must consider how the AFL and its clubs can maintain some sense of community for its members and fans. In considering this, we must also acknowledge that the influence of capitalism and neoliberalism in the AFL appears irreversible. In today's professional era of sport, few Australians, if any, expect their elite athletes to perform without some form of payment. Nor do Australians expect the AFL to reject an economic rationalist model totally, for to do so is to expect them to ignore corporate sponsorships, advertisements and broadcasting rights deals, which are now part and parcel of the sport and, even more significantly, fundamental to its survival. Reversing the trend also requires hundreds of AFL coaches to disappear, components of AFL elite sport programs to dissolve and players to ignore lucrative contracts from other sport to play Australian football simply for the love of the game. So, to suggest that the play element can somehow return to its pure, ideal form in order to stimulate genuine community is unrealistic.

But this does not mean that the AFL and its clubs cannot play a role in ensuring the game of Australian football continues to create a sense of community within society. It does not mean that they can't help ensure that the play element in the AFL reflects the play element that existed at the game's founding, which is still alive and well at the grassroots level of the sport today. To do this, the AFL must focus on the two key areas of the game that have served as the basis of this book: play and community:

The play element
The fans interviewed for this study highlighted that the play element within the AFL is at times unrecognisable in terms of what it was twenty years ago and of what it still is at the grassroots, suburban and country levels of football today. Therefore, AFL must ensure that it acts as a regulator of the game, on behalf of the fans and must make necessary rule changes to ensure the best qualities of the game – the high marks, the long runs, the spectacular goals, the one on one contests – remain defining features of the game.

The coaches
Because coaches are mostly interested in winning, they have changed the style of play to gain a competitive edge against their opponents, regardless of the impact their tactics have on the aesthetics of the game or, indeed, on the areas of the game from which the fans derive the most enjoyment. Therefore, the AFL needs to ensure that the fans remain the custodians of the game and the way it is played. They must regularly source the fans views and opinions about the game and act on their feedback to make necessary changes. They cannot allow coaches to be the dominating factor of determining how the game is played. That role should sit with the fans.

Fan engagement
The AFL must also focus on the game's community. The responses of the interview participants highlighted that the AFL's communities have been weakened as the game has become more professional and commercial. Fans don't feel they are able to influence the game or the clubs they support. Furthermore, other than purchasing memberships, few are active in helping clubs achieve their goals.

To change this trend, the AFL must look for new ways to engage their fans in a manner that provides them with a voice and real influence, while encouraging an active contribution to the shared and common goals of the club. To do this, the AFL and its clubs should enhance their use of digital and social media. Currently, the league and its clubs use social media channels to promote themselves, provide members and fans with information about the clubs and players and produce content they believe their social media followers will find entertaining. Thus, their social media use appears more an act of marketing and promotion than meaningful engagement with the community.

As physical communities decline within AFL clubs, online communities must provide more than entertaining content and use social media as part of a broader strategy to ensure the fans remain the number one stakeholders of the game. The league and its clubs can use these forms of communication to obtain meaningful feedback about their clubs, the AFL and the play element. They can consult with members about pending decisions the clubs face and respond to fans regarding the use of their feedback in the decision-making process. They can also encourage members of their online communities to engage with their clubs physically as well as virtually. That is, the league and its clubs should encourage fans to meet at free club events, coming together to enjoy something in common with others and forming personal ties with other members of the community.

The broader community

Furthermore, the AFL should encourage fans and members to participate in society and to make active contributions to enrich their communities. Most of the interview respondents claimed they felt a more distinct sense of community when engaged with their local football clubs. Rather than be threatened by this, the AFL must not only embrace it but assist it. Although the league does invest in grassroots and junior football, many younger AFL fans are choosing to consume AFL football through the passive observation of elite athletes participating in play. Therefore, the AFL should prioritise investment in grassroots and community forms of the game to ensure participation continues to increase. Through such a focus, the AFL will not only stimulate genuine play but also uphold the characteristics of community and ensure fans of Australian football feel a genuine sense of community.

In addition, from a broader strategic perspective, the AFL must resist the temptation to rationalise the competition across Australia fully by ensuring all Victorian teams continue in their current forms, with their training base and club headquarters located in or close to, their original suburb. Doing so will help guarantee some sense of tribalism and club support based upon historical family and community ties.

Growth

The AFL should look towards Tasmania to form its next club, a club that will emerge from the shared passion and uprising of the community. By doing so, the AFL will give Tasmanians the opportunity to come together to enjoy the game they've loved for over 150 years.

Ensuring strong participation at the junior, grassroots and community level of suburban and country football, the AFL will not only maintain its fan base but also win new fans to the game, all the while ensuring they feel a genuine sense of community stimulated through the game of Australian football. The AFL and its clubs can actively encourage and promote this through programs such as their community camps and through increased investment in grass roots football.

Conclusion

Australians love their footy and seemingly have an unquenchable thirst for the game. The game has been an integral part of their lives from birth. It is 'the most exciting, exhilarating and unpredictable spectator sport',[2] 'the best game in the world'.[3] Being a club member provides a 'sense of identity',[4] 'a sense of pride and belonging',[5] where 'in some small way you're a part of it'.[6] However, the merger of the economic, media and sport fields has changed the game significantly over the last thirty years in ways that have affected not only the play element but also the sense of community engendered through the game. Thus, Australian football at the elite level is a shadow of what the people's game was at its founding.

The professionalisation of the sport has produced a game that is quite different from its origins, transforming it from a game in which the people participated actively, both on the field and in the club house, to one in which fans participate more passively, barracking for one's team in the grandstands, watching games on television, consuming media programs and broadcasts, and contributing financially through club memberships to assist the club in achieving its goal of winning the Grand Final.

Although little can be done to reverse the professionalisation of the game, the AFL can still ensure the characteristics of community that still exist at the grassroots level of the game are afforded to its members, supporters and fans. By ensuring the play element in the AFL maintains some form of its original characteristics of freedom, spontaneity and flair, the AFL will ensure fans of all ages still have opportunities to come together to enjoy a game characterised by high marks, long kicks and spectacular goals. By utilising social media to provide fans with a meaningful voice and genuine channels of influence, the AFL will give fans a sense of meaning that they can attach to their annual membership. By encouraging fans of Australian football to participate actively within junior, suburban and country football clubs, as well as supporting the elite level of competition, the AFL will encourage citizens to contribute actively in helping their local clubs reach their goals.

In taking these steps, the AFL will help ensure that Australian football continues to play a vital role in creating and strengthening communities at all levels of society. Thus, Australian football will remain the people's game, the game of the people for the people.

Notes

Introduction

1. For studies about the commercialisation of the game, see Stephen Alomes, *Australian Football: The People's Game 1958–2058*; and Bernard East, *Australian Rules Football in a Commercial Era – Catering for Theatregoers and Tribals*. For studies about AFL fans and fan culture, see Matthew Klugman, *Passion Play: Love, Hope and Heartbreak at the Footy*; and John Cash and Joy Damousi, *Footy Passions*. For more about the concept of AFL communities, see Ian Andrews, 'The Transformation of "Community" in the AFL, Part One: Towards a Conceptual Framework for "Community"' and 'Redrawing "Community" Boundaries in the Post-War AFL'; Dave Nadel, 'What is a Football Community?'.

2. Sasha Orive, *Victorian Rules: Populi Ludos Populo – The Game of the People for the People*. Originally the motto of the Victorian Football League, *populo ludus populi* is now the motto of the AFL.

Chapter 1

1. Stephen Alomes, *A Nation at Last?: The Changing Character of Australian Nationalism 1880–1988*, 16.

2. Helen Irving, *To Constitute a Nation: A Cultural History of Australia's Constitution*, 33.

3. Geoffrey Blainey, *A Game of Our Own: The Origins of Australian Football*, 17–18.

4. Anne Mancini and Gillian M. Hibbins, *Running with the Ball: Football's Foster Father*, 21.

5. Blainey, *A Game of Our Own*, 17–18.

6. 'Sport: Touchstone of Australian Life', *The Sports Factor*.

7. Martin Flanagan, *The Call*, 8.

8. Robert Brough Smyth, *The Aborigines of Victoria: With Notes Relating to the Habits of the Natives of Other Parts of Australia and Tasmania*, 176.

9. Ibid.

10. Flanagan, *The Call*, 8.

11. Richard Cashman, 'Australian Sport and Culture before Federation', in *Sport, History and Australian Culture*, 30.

12. Jenny Hocking and Nell Reidy, 'Marngrook, Tom Wills and the Continuing Denial of Indigenous History: On the Origins of Australian Football'.

13. Gillian Hibbins, cited in James Weston (ed.), *The Australian Game of Football*, 76.

14. Weston (ed.), *The Australian Game of Football*, 14.

15. Cashman, 'Australian Sport and Culture before Federation', 29.

16. Bill Murray, *Introduction to Football: A History of the World Game*, xiii–xiv.

17. Margaret Lindsay, 'Taking the Joke Too Far and Footballers' Shorts', in *Gender, Sexuality and Sport: A Dangerous Mix*, 66.

18. Ibid., 65.

19. Ibid., 66.

20. Mark Pennings, *Origins of Australian Football: Victoria's Early History: Volume 1: Amateur Heroes and the Rise of Clubs, 1858 to 1876*.

21. Blainey, *A Game of Our Own*, 64–65.

22. Robert Hess, 'Women and Australian Rules Football in Colonial Melbourne', 356.

23. The exact date of the club's formation is unknown. However, the club played its first recorded game in June 1873 against a Carlton side.

24. Essendon Football Club, 'Club History'.

25. Ibid.

26. 'History of Windy Hill, Essendon'.

27. Michael Maplestone, *Flying Higher: History of the Essendon Football Club 1872–1995*, 40.

28. Ibid., 12.

29. Garrie Hutchison, 'How the Teams Got Their Names', in *100 Years of Australian Football 1897–1996: The Complete Story of the AFL, All the Big Stories, All the Great Pictures, All the Champions, Every AFL Season Reported*. 159.

30. Essendon Football Club, 'Club History'.

31. Mark Pennings, 'Fuchsias, Pivots, Same Olds and Gorillas: The Early Years of Football in Victoria', 5.

32. Ibid., 160.

33. John Rickard, *An Assemblage of Decent Men and Women: A History of the Anglican Parish of St Mary's North Melbourne 1853–2000*, 4–5.

34. Ron Joseph, 'North Melbourne Football Club Best and Fairest'.

35. Graeme Atkinson, *Everything You Ever Wanted to Know about Australian Rules Football*, 47.

36. Blainey, *A Game of Our Own*, 74–75.

37. 'AFL History'.

38. Riosin Grow, in Weston (ed.), *The Australian Game of Football since 1858*, 56.

39. Ibid., 56.

40. Ibid.

41. Ibid., 57.

42. Trevor Grant, 'Battle Grounds', 20.

43. Ibid.

44. Johan Huizinga, *Homo Ludens: A Study of the Play-Element in Culture*, 1950 [1938].

45. Paul Daffey, 'A Wonderful Tradition'.

46. Jeff Dowsing, 'Era, Era on the Wall: 1949–1959', Part 3 – Safe at Home, and Away.

47. 'Chronology of Australian Football'.

48. Ibid.

49. Ibid.

50. Ibid.

51. 'NAB Draft Hub'.

52. 'AFL History'.

53. Blainey, *A Game of Our Own*, 76.

Chapter 2

1. Johan Huizinga, *Homo Ludens: A Study of the Play-Element in Culture* (1949), 2.
2. Ibid., 8–10.
3. Ibid., 49.
4. Ibid.
5. Ibid.
6. Ibid.
7. David Boucher, 'Practical Hegelianism: Henry Jones's Lecture Tour of Australia', 423; David Boucher and A. Vincent, *British Idealism: A Guide for the Perplexed*; Arran Gare, 'The Neoliberal Assault on Australian Universities and the Future of Democracy: The Philosophical Failure of a Nation', 21–41; Marian Sawer, *The Ethical State? Social Liberalism in Australia*, 44.
8. Georg Hegel, *Philosophy of Right* (1952), 153f (section 253); also see Georg Hegel, *Philosophy of Right* (1967).
9. Huizinga, *Homo Ludens* (1950), 11.
10. Jane Jacobs, *The Death and Life of Great American Cities*, 147.
11. Robert Putnam, 'Bowling Alone: America's Declining Social Capital', 65–78.
12. Robert Putnam, *Bowling Alone, The Collapse and Revival of American Community*, 61.
13. Robert Putnam, *Making Democracy Work: Civic Traditions in Modern Italy*, 130.
14. Ibid.
15. Ibid., 177.
16. Ferdinand Tönnies, *Community and Society*.
17. Ibid., 15.
18. See Erving Goffman, *Interaction Ritual: Essays on Face to Face Behaviour*; Travis Hirschi, *Causes of Delinquency*; Rosabeth Moss Kanter, *Commitment and Community: Communes and Utopias in Sociological*; William Julius Wilson, *The Truly Disadvantaged: The Inner City, the Underclass and Public Policy.* Goffmann, Hirschi, Kanter and Wilson followed the work of Emile Durkheim (1893), who saw community as a set of variables rather than as essential properties. For more detail see Emile Durkheim, *The Division of Labour in Society*; Emile Durkheim, *Suicide*.
19. Ian Andrews, 'The Transformation of "Community" in the AFL Part One: Towards a Conceptual Framework for "Community"', 106.
20. Dave Nadel, 'What is a Football Community?'
21. Benedict Anderson, *Imagined Communities: Reflections on the Origin and Spread of Nationalism*.
22. Thomas Bender, *Community and social change in America*, 6–7.
23. David McMillan and David Chavis, 'Sense of Community, A definition and theory', 6–23.
24. Key contributors to the concept of social community include the following: David McMillan and David Chavis, 'Sense of Community, A Definition and Theory', 6–23; Grace Pretty, 'Sense of Community: Advances in Measurement and Application', 635–42; Joseph R. Gusfield, *The Community: A Critical Response*; Stephanie Riger and Paul J. Lavrakas, 'Community Ties: Patterns of Attachment and Social Interaction in Urban Neighbourhoods', 55–66;

Seymour Sarason, 'Commentary: The Emergence of a Conceptual Center', 405–7; Seymour Sarason, *The Psychological Sense of Community: Prospects for a Community Psychology*.

25. McMillan and Chavis are two of the most validated and widely utilised contributors on these elements of sense of community in the psychological literature.

26. Stephen Alomes, 'The Lie of the Ground: Aesthetics and Australian Football'.

27. Thomas Hill Green, 'Lecture on "Liberal Legislation and Freedom of Contract"', 199.

28. Hegel, *Philosophy of Right* (1952).

29. Green, 'Lecture on "Liberal Legislation and Freedom of Contract"', 199.

30. Walter Murdoch, *The Australian Citizen: An Elementary Account of Civic Rights and Duties*, 8. See also Marilyn Lake, *Alfred Deakin's Dream of Independence*.

31. Donald W. Winnicott, *Playing and Reality*, 74.

32. Ibid., 75.

Chapter 3

1. Tom O'Regan, *Australian Television Culture*, 40.

2. Ibid., 59.

3. Pierre Bourdieu, 'The Forms of Capital', 241–60.

4. Ibid., 245.

5. Pierre Bourdieu, 'Structures, Habitus, Practices', 52.

6. Bourdieu, 'The Forms of Capital'. See also Pierre Bourdieu, *The Field of Cultural Production: Essay Is Art and Literature*; Pierre Bourdieu, *The Rules of Art: Genesis and Structure of the Literary Field*; Pierre Bourdieu and J. Passeron, 'Cultural Reproduction and Social Reproduction', 56–68.

7. Bourdieu, 'The Forms of Capital', 246.

8. Huizinga, *Homo Ludens* (1950), 16.

9. Stuart Osbourne, interview with author, 20 May 2013. All other statements from Stuart Osbourne were taken from the interview conducted on 20 May 2013. See appendix for a complete list of AFL fans interviewed as part of my research.

10. Alanna Ford, interview with author, 8 September 2015. All other statements from Alanna Ford were taken from the interview conducted on 8 September 2015.

11. Huizinga, *Homo Ludens* (1950), 177.

12. Ibid., 192.

13. Ibid., 74.

14. Ibid., 75.

15. Ibid., 13.

16. David Rowe, 'Understanding Sport and Media: A Socio-Historical Approach', 20.

17. Ibid.

18. Johan Huizinga, *Homo Ludens* (1950), 196.

19. Ibid., 204.

20. Ibid., 195.

21. Christopher Lasch, *The Culture of Narcissism: American Life in an Age of Diminishing Expectations*, 57.

22. Ibid., 58–59.

23. Ibid., 59.

24. Ibid., 61

25. Ibid., 62–63.

26. Ibid., 60.

27. Huizinga, *Homo Ludens* (1950).

28. Thomas Frank, *One Market under God: Extreme Capitalism, Market Populism and the End of Economic Democracy*, 95.

29. Ibid., 98.

30. Viola Spolin, *Improvisation for the Theatre*, 11.

31. Huizinga, *Homo Ludens* (1950), 30.

32. Jean Baudrillard, *The Precession of Simulacra*, 4.

Chapter 4

1. Gillon McLachlan, 'AFL CEO Gillon McLachlan's Statement on New Broadcast Deal'.

2. Travis Auld, 'AFL Clubs and Operations'.

3. Styles, Aja. 'AFL Grand Final 2016 has highest footy ratings for Channel 7 in a decade'.

4 'How Much Does It Cost to Get an NRL and AFL Grand Final TV Advertising Spot?'

5. Auld, 'AFL Clubs and Operations'.

6. Kate Withers, interview with author, 31 August 2015. All other statements from Kate Withers were taken from the interview conducted on 31 August 2015.

7. Steve Sleight, *Sponsorship: What It Is and How to Use It*, 199.

8. Zak Kardachi, interview with author, 23 May 2013. All other statements from Zak Kardachi were taken from the interview conducted on 23 May 2013.

9. John Goldlust, *Playing for Keeps*, 91.

10. As cited in Caroline Wilson, 'Roos Fuming at Ten's Commentary', 89.

11. Tim Watson, interview with author, 15 September 2007. All other statements from Tim Watson were taken from the interview conducted on 15 September 2007.

12. Rex Hunt, interview with author, 10 October 2007. All other statements from Rex Hunt were taken from the interview conducted on 10 October 2007.

13. The media covered this issue extensively in 2006. See Caroline Wilson, 'Fair Call? No Way Say Clubs' Chief Executives'.

14. Scott Hutchins, interview with author, 22 May 2013. All other statements from Scott Hutchins were taken from the interview conducted 22 May 2013.

15. For details of other clubs' football department spending, see the clubs' annual reports. Also see Greg Denham and Patrick Smith, 'AFL's Great Money Divide May Finally Be Shrinking'.

16. Michael Westland, interview with author, 16 May 2013. All other statements from Michael Westland taken from the interview conducted 16 May 2013.

17. For overview an of total player payments in the AFL, see Andrew Dillon and Brett Clothier, 'Legal and Integrity'.

18. Jeremiah Ryan, interview with author, 6 June 2013. All other statements from Jeremiah Ryan were taken from the interview conducted 6 June 2013.

19. Cheree Brown, interview with author, 10 September 2015. All other statements from Cheree Brown were taken from the interview conducted 10 September 2015.

20. 'The AFL's Equalisation Policy Explained'.
21. Ibid.
22. Ibid.
23. Ibid.
24. Peter Di Sisto, interview with author, 14 March 2006. All other statements from Peter Di Sisto were taken from the interview conducted 14 March 2006.
25. Huizinga, *Homo Ludens* (1950).

Chapter 5

1. Huizinger, *Homo Ludens* (1950).
2. As cited in Trevor Grant, 'The Reluctant Star', 10–11.
3. Ibid.
4. James Hird, 'Home Is Where the Heart and Soul Is', 90.
5. Huizinga, *Homo Ludens* (1950), 13.
6. John Devaney, Western Bulldogs, in 'Australian Football: Celebrating the History of the Great Australian Game'.
7. John Devaney, North Melbourne, in 'Australian Football: Celebrating the History of the Great Australian Game'.
8. For more information about the history of each club, see 'Australian Football: Celebrating the History of the Great Australian Game'.
9. Hawthorn Football Club, Annual Financial Report: Year Ending 31 October 2007.
10. Heath O'Loughlin, 'History: North in Hobart'.
11. Ibid.
12. 'AFL Rules – Laws of the Game 2015'.
13. Huizinga, *Homo Ludens* (1950).
14. 'NAB Fantasy'.
15. John Devaney, Carlton, in 'Australian Football: Celebrating the History of the Great Australian Game'.
16. Ibid.
17. Adrian Anderson, 'Football Operations'.
18. Greg Denham, 'Karmichael Hunt Turns His Back on NRL Offers to Extend His Time with the Suns'. Even though AFL clubs do not disclose how much they pay individual players, the AFL media reported Hunt's contract details.
19. Mike Colman, 'AFL Hangs League Convert Karmichael Hunt Out to Dry'.
20. Sophie Elsworth, 'Gary Ablett Jnr Signs Deal with Gold Coast Suns'; Caroline Wilson and Will Brodie, 'Footy's Favourite Son Rises to Gold Coast Challenge'.
21. Adrian Anderson, 'Football Operations'. The salary cap for the Gold Coast Suns is still higher than most other clubs.
22. Tom Gallimore, interview with author, 21 May 2013. All other statements from Tom Gallimore were taken from the interview conducted 21 May 2013.
23. Effie Caloutas, interview with author, 1 September 2015. All other statements from Effie Caloutas were taken from the interview conducted 1 September 2015.
24. Michael Cowley and Sean Baumgart, 'Revealed: How Kevin Sheedy and GWS Got Their Man', 89.
25. Brian Walsh, 'Corporate Affairs and Communications'.

26. Lou Lando, 'Israel Folau Is Doomed to Fail with GWS Giants'

27. Jason Lee, interview with author, 13 June 2013. All other statements from Jason Lee were taken from the interview conducted 13 June 2013.

28. Phil Wild interview with author, 28 May 2013. All other statements from Phil Wild were taken from the interview conducted 28 May 2013.

29. Josh Forte, interview with author, 30 May 2013. All other statements from Josh Forte were taken from the interview conducted 30 May 2013.

30. Hunt and Folau have both since defected from the AFL to rugby union.

31. 'Free Agency'.

32. Jon Ralph, 'No Looking Back', 106.

33. Phil Wild.

34. Huizinga, *Homo Ludens* (1950), 13.

35. Ibid., 51.

36. Cited in Trevor Grant, 'The Reluctant Star', 10.

Chapter 6

1. 'AFL Rules – Laws of the Game 2013'.

2. 'The Brownlow Medal Hub'.

3. 'AFL Draft'.

4. Oxford Dictionaries, s.v. 'tank'.

5. Huizinga, *Homo Ludens* (1950), 7.

6. Brock Mclean, 'On the Couch: Interview with Brock Mclean'.

7. 'A Full Statement: Melbourne Tanking Penalties'.

8. Ibid.

9. 'Full Statement from Essendon Chairman David Evans'.

10. 'Human Growth Hormone (HGH) Directory'.

11. World Anti-Doping Agency (WADA), *The 2013 Prohibited List: International Standard*. Also see WADA, *The 2012 Prohibited List: International Standard*.

12. Ashley Browne, 'Bomber Shocker – The Key Questions'.

13. Court of Arbitration for Sport, *CAS 2015/A/4059 World Anti-Doping Agency v. Thomas Bellchambers et al., Australian Football League, Australian Sports Anti-Doping Authority Arbitral Award*.

14. Ibid.

15. Matt Thompson and Nathan Schmook, 'Essendon 34 appeal confirmed as players seek to clear their names'.

16. Australian Crime Commission (ACC), Organised Cr 191 ime and Drugs in Sport: New Generation Performance and Image Enhancing Drugs and Organised Crime Involvement in Their Use in Professional Sport.

17. Ibid., 17.

18. Ibid.

19. Ibid., 8.

20. Ibid., 25.

21. Ibid.

22. Ibid.

23. Ibid., 26.

24. Ibid., 27.

25. Ibid.

26. Ibid., 28.

27. Ibid., 34.

28. Ibid., 31.

29. Ibid., 31

30. 'Full Statement from the AFL'.

31. Cambridge Dictionaries Online, s.v. match-fixing.

32. Oxford Dictionaries, s.v. match-fixing.

33. ACC, Organised Crime and Drugs in Sport.

34. 'Full Statement from the AFL'.

Chapter 7

1. Paul Daffey, foreword to *Footy Town: Stories of Australia's Game*, 1.

2. Ibid., 2.

3. Ibid., 3.

4. Lionel Frost, Margaret Lightbody, and Abdel Halabi, 'Expanding Social Inclusion in Community Sport Organisations: Evidence from Rural Australian Football Clubs'.

5. Ibid., 30.

6. Ibid.

7. Ibid. See also N. Richardson, 'Saturday Night Replay: How the Sporting Globe Came to Change Australian Rules Football in Victoria during the 1920s', 121.

8. Daffey, foreword, 2.

9. Neil Duncan, interview with author, 15 May 2013. All other statements from Neil Duncan were taken from the interview conducted 15 May 2013.

10. A. Hughes, 'The Jewish Community', 103.

11. Barry Markoff, *The Road to 'A' Grade: A History of the Ajax Football Club*, 14.

12. Ibid., 15.

13. Andrew Demetriou, 'CEO's Report'.

14. Markoff, *The Road to 'A' Grade*.

15. Paul Daffey, *Local Rites*.

16. Robert Hess and Bob Stewart (eds), *More than A Game: An Unauthorised History of Australian Rules Football*.

17. Ibid., 11.

18. Stephen Alomes, *Australian Football: The People's Game 1958–2058*, 100.

19. Roslyn Lanigan, 'How Much Is Your Local Footy Team Worth?'.

20. Ibid.

21. Alomes, *Australian Football*, 102.

22. Frost et al., 'Expanding Social Inclusion in Community Sport Organisations', 14.

23. Ibid., 15.

24. 'AFL, 2015 Highlights', 10.

25. Simon Lethlean, 'Game and Market Development' 84–91.

26. Essendon Football Club, 'Community'.

27. Ibid.

28. Ibid.

29. Ibid.

Chapter 8

1. Michael Pusey, *Integrity under Stress: Economic Rationalism in Canberra – A Nation Building State Changes Its Mind*, 208.

2. Manfred Steger and Ravi Roy, *Neoliberalism: A Very Short Introduction*, 21–49.

3. Pusey, *Integrity under Stress*.

4. Steger and Roy, *Neoliberalism*.

5. Sawer, *The Ethical State?*, 44; Walter Murdoch, *Loose Leaves*, 64f.

6. Green, 'Lecture on "Liberal

Legislation and Freedom of Contract'", 199.

7. Steger and Roy, *Neoliberalism*, 119–37.

8. Euclid Tsakalotos, 'Social Norms and Endogenous Preferences: The Political Economy of Market Expansion', 5–6.

9. Pusey, *Integrity under Stress*, 232.

10. Steger and Roy, *Neoliberalism*, 138.

11. United Nations Conference on Trade and Development, The Global Economic Crisis: Systemic Failures and Multilateral Remedies.

12. Kevin Rudd, 'The Global Financial Crisis'.

13. R.K. Stewart, introduction to 'The Economic Development of the Victorian Football League 1960–1984'.

14. John Devaney, Sydney, in 'Australian Football: Celebrating the History of the Great Australian Game'.

15. Ibid.

16. Matthew Nicholson, 'Print Media Representation of Crisis Events in Australian Football, 111.

17. Ibid.

18. Ibid., 120–21.

19. Ibid., 132.

20. Ibid., 128

21. Ron Reed, 'Swans Sparks 258 but No Flair', 41.

22. Ibid.

23. Nicholson, 'Print Media Representation of Crisis Events in Australian Football', 122.

24. Mike Sheahan, 'South Needs Compromise', 52.

25. Nicholson, 'Print Media Representation of Crisis Events in Australian Football', 140–41.

26. See the following for accounts of South Melbourne's relocation to Sydney: Mark Branagan and Mike Lefebvre, *Bloodstained Angels: The Rise and Fall of the Foreign Legion*; Jim Main, *In the Blood: South Melbourne–Sydney Swans Football Club*; Kevin Taylor, *The Sydney Swans: The Complete History, 1874–1986*.

27. 'AFL History'.

28. AFL, *AFL Record Season Guide*.

29. John Devaney, Fitzroy, in 'Australian Football: Celebrating the History of the Great Australian Game'.

30. Ibid.

31. Nicholson, 'Print Media Representation of Crisis Events in Australian Football', ch. 6.

32. Ibid.

33. Ibid., ch. 5.

34. Ibid.

35. Ibid., 284. Also see Garrie Hutchison and John Ross, *Roar of the Lions, Fitzroy Remembered 1883–1996*; Dave Nadel, 'The Professionalisation and Commercialisation of Australian Football, 1975–1996'; Bob Stewart, *The Australian Football Business*.

36. Department of Economic Development, Tourism and the Arts, 'A History of Football in Tasmania'.

37. Ibid.

38. Hawthorn Football Club, Annual Financial Report; North Melbourne Football Club, 'New Power for North'.

39. Hawthorn Football Club, Hawthorn FC Membership.

40. Department of Economic Development, Tourism and the Arts, '10 Reasons Tassie Should Have an AFL Team'.

41. Cited in Department of Economic Development, Tourism and the Arts, 'Messages of Support'.

42. Ibid.

43. Department of Economic Development, Tourism and the Arts, 'Bi 280 d Criter_a'.

44. Zak Kardachi.

Chapter 9

1. Ten interviews were conducted in 2013 as part of a research project (see Samuel Duncan, 'How the Play Element Has Changed in Australian Football and the Consequences of This Change on Community', (unpublished doctoral thesis, Swinburne University of Technology, Hawthorn, Victoria, 2015). These individuals were selected through a convenience sampling technique, resulting in all participants being male. To balance the information from interviewees for this work, I interviewed four female AFL fans in 2015. The appendix contains a list of all fourteen individuals and the dates of their interviews.

2. Zak Kardachi.

3. Johan Huizinga, *Men and Ideas: History, the Middle Ages, the Renaissance: Essays by Johan Huizinga*, 39.

4. Cheree Brown.

5. Frank, *One Market under God*, 92.

6. Baudrillard, *The Precession of Simulacra*.

Chapter 10

1. Michel Desbordes, *Marketing and Football: An International Perspective*, 98.

2. Sourav Das, 'Top 10 Highest Paid Soccer Players 2015'.

3. Fédération Internationale de Football Association (FIFA), Laws of the Game 2012/2013.

4. David Conn, *The Beautiful Game? Searching the Soul of Football*, 54.

5. See 'NAB Draft Hub'.

6. 'English Premier League TV Deal: Sky and BR Outlay $10 Billion in Stunning Three-Season EPL Outlay'.

7. Alan Tomlinson and Christopher Young, *National Identity and Global Sports Events: Culture, Politics and Spectacle in the Olympics and the Football World*.

Chapter 11

1. AFL, '2015 Highlights', 4–7.

2. Auld, 'AFL Clubs and Operations'.

3. Angus Grigg, 'Gentleman's Code', 60.

4. Darren Birch, 'Commercial Operations'.

5. Collingwood Football Club, Annual Financial Report 2011.

6. Cited in Grigg, 'Gentleman's Code', 70.

7. Ray Gunstan, 'Financial Report'.

8. Andrew Demetriou, 'An Ongoing Challenge'.

9. Gillon McLachlan and Simon Lethlean, 'Broadcasting, Scheduling and Infrastructure'.

10. Brian Walsh, 'Growing Coverage Spreads Game's Appeal'.

11. *Herald Sun*, 9 December 2011.

12. Auld, 'AFL Clubs and Operations', 44.

13. McLachlan, 'AFL CEO Gillon McLachlan's Statement on New Broadcast Deal'.

14. Ray Gunstan, 'Financial Report', 138–139, 1 June 2016.

15. Huizinga, *Homo Ludens* (1950).

Chapter 12

1. Huizinga, *Homo Ludens* (1950).
2. Kate Withers.
3. Cheree Brown.
4. Alanna Ford.
5. Kate Withers.
6. Jason Lee.

Bibliography

AFL, *AFL Record Season Guide*. Melbourne: Slattery Media, 2012.

AFL, '2015 Highlights'. In *Australian Football League Annual Report 2015*, accessed 1 June 2016, Ray Gunston, 'Financial Report', in *Australian Football League Annual Report 2015*, 138–139, 1 June, 2016, http://s.afl.com.au/staticfile/AFL%20Tenant/AFL/Files/Annual%20Report/AFLAnnualReport2015.pdf.

'AFL Draft', AFL Rules, accessed 5 May 2013, http://www.aflrules.com.au/afl-players/afl-draft/.

'AFL History'. AFL.com, accessed May 2013, www.afl.com.au/AFLHQ/History/tabid/967/Default.aspx.

'AFL Rules – Laws of the Game 2015', AFL.com, accessed 9 September 2015 http://www.afl.com.au/afl-hq/laws-of-the-game.

'The AFL's Equalisation Policy Explained', AFL com, accessed 6 March 2014, http://www.afl.com.au/news/2014-05-04/equalisation-changes-explained.

Alomes, Stephen. *Australian Football: The People's Game 1958–2058*. Sydney: Walla Walla Press, 2012.

Alomes, Stephen. 'The Lie of the Ground: Aesthetics and Australian Football'. *Double Dialogues*, no. 8 (Summer 2007), accessed 27 April 2013, http://www.doubledialogues.com/article/the-lie-of-the-ground-aesthetics-and-australian-football/.

Alomes, Stephen. *A Nation at Last? The Changing Character of Australian Nationalism 1880–1988*. North Ryde, NSW: Angus and Robertson, 1988.

Anderson, Adrian. 'Football Operations'. In AFL, Annual Report 2012, 50–63, accessed 19 October 2015, http://s.afl.com.au/staticfile/AFL%20Tenant/AFL/Files/AFL%20Annual%20Report%202012_web.pdf.

Anderson, Ian. 'Financial Report'. In AFL, *Australian Football League Annual Report 2013*, 145–149, accessed 6 March 2014, http://www.afl.com.au/staticfile/AFL%20Tenant/AFL/Files/Annual%20Report/2013%2AFL%20Annual%20Report.pdf.

Andrews, Ian. 'The Transformation of "Community" in the AFL Part One: Towards a Conceptual Framework for 'Community', in *Occasional Papers in Football Studies*, Vol. 1, No. 2, 1998.

Andrews, Ian. 'Redrawing 'Community' Boundaries in the Post-War AFL', in *Occasional Papers in Football Studies*, Vol. 2, No. 1, 1999.

Atkinson, Graeme. *Everything You Ever Wanted to Know about Australian Rules Football*. Melbourne: Five Mile Press, 1982.

Auld, Travis. 'AFL Clubs and Operations' in *Australian Football League Annual Report 2015*, accessed 1 June 2016, http://s.afl.

com.au/staticfile/AFL%20Tenant/AFL/Files/Annual%20Report/AFLAnnualReport2015.pdf.

Australian Crime Commission (ACC). Organised Crime and Drugs in Sport: New Generation Performance and Image Enhancing Drugs and Organised Crime Involvement in Their Use in Professional Sport. Canberra City: Author, 2013, accessed 2 March 2014, https://www.crimecommission.gov.au/sites/default/files/organised-crime-and-drugs-in-sport-feb2013.pdf.

'Australian Football: Celebrating the History of the Great Australian Game', AustralianFootball.com, accessed 28 March 2013, http://australianfootball.com/clubs

Baudrillard, Jean. *The Precession of Simulacra*. New York: Semiotexte, 1983.

Bender, Thomas. *Community and social change in America*. Baltimore: John Hopkins University Press, 1978.

Birch, Darren. 'Commercial Operations'. In AFL, Australian Football League Report 2015, accessed 1 June 2016, http://s.afl.com.au/staticfile/AFL%20Tenant/AFL/Files/Annual%20Report/AFLAnnualReport2015.pdf.

Blainey, Geoffrey. *A Game of Our Own: The Origins of Australian Football*. Melbourne: Information Australia, 1990.

Boucher, David. 'Practical Hegelianism: Henry Jones's Lecture Tour of Australia'. *Journal of the History of Ideas* 51, no. 3 (1990): 423–52.

Boucher, David, and A. Vincent. *British Idealism: A Guide for the Perplexed*. London: Bloomsbury, 2011.

Bourdieu, Pierre. *The Field of Cultural Production: Essay Is Art and Literature*. New York: Columbia University Press, 1993.

Bourdieu, Pierre. 'The Forms of Capital'. In *Handbook of Theory and Research for the Sociology of Education*, edited by J. G. Richardson, 241–61. New York: Greenwood Press, 1986.

Bourdieu, Pierre. *The Rules of Art: Genesis and Structure of the Literary Field*. Stanford: Stanford University Press, 1996.

Bourdieu, Pierre. 'Structures, Habitus, Practices'. In *The Logic of Practice*, trans. Richard Nice, 52–66. Stanford: Stanford University Press, 1990.

Bourdieu, Pierre, and Jean Claude Passeron. 'Cultural Reproduction and Social Reproduction'. In *Knowledge, Education and Cultural Change*, edited by Robert Brown, 56–68. London: Tavistock, 1973.

Branagan, Mark, and Mike Lefebvre. *Bloodstained Angels: The Rise and Fall of the Foreign Legion*. Melbourne: Author, 1995.

Browne, Ashley. 'Bomber Shocker – The Key Questions'. *AFL News*, 6 February 2013, accessed 6 February 2013, www.afl.com.au/news/2013-02-06/bomber-shocker-the-key-questions.

'The Brownlow Medal Hub'. AFL.com, accessed 5 May 2013, http://www.afl.com.au/news/event-news/brownlow/about-the-brownlow.

Caillois, Rodger 'The Definition of Play and The Classification of Games'. In Salen, K., and E. Zimmerman, *The Game Design Reader: A Rules of Play Anthology*. Boston, Massachusetts Institute of Technology, 2006

Campbell, Peter. 'AFL Media', in

Australian Football League Annual Report 2015, accessed 1 June 2016, http://s.afl.com.au/staticfile/AFL%20Tenant/AFL/Files/Annual%20Report/AFLAnnualReport2015.pdf.

Cash, John and Damousi, Joy. *Footy Passions*. Sydney: University of NSW Press, 2009.

Cashman, Richard. 'Australian Sport and Culture before Federation'. In *Sport, History and Australian Culture*, edited by Richard Cashman and Robert Hess, 30. Sydney: Walla Wall Press, 2011.

Chavis, David M., and Grace Pretty. 'Sense of Community: Advances in Measurement and Application'. *Journal of Community Psychology* 27, no. 6 (1999): 635–42.

'Chronology of Australian Football'. AFL.com, accessed 19 October 2015, http://www.afl.com.au/afl-hq/the-afl-explained/chronology.

Collingwood Football Club. Annual Financial Report 2011, accessed 5 May 2013, http://www.collingwoodfc.com.au/staticfile/AFL%20Tenant/Collingwood/Club%20Promos/2012%20-%20Club%20Promos/2011_CFC_annual_report.pdf.

Colman, Mike. AFL Hangs League Convert Karmichael Hunt Out to Dry'. *Sunday Mail*, 16 August 2009.

Conn, David. *The Beautiful Game? Searching the Soul of Football*. London: Random House 2005.

Court of Arbitration for Sport, CAS 2015/A/4059 World Anti-Doping Agency v. Thomas Bellchambers et al., Australian Football League. Australian Sports Anti-Doping Authority Arbitral Award. Lausanne. Court of Arbitration for Sport, accessed 6 October 2016, http://www.tas-cas.org.fileadmin/user_upload/Arbitral_Award_WADA_ESSENDON.pdf, 45.

Cowley, Michael, and Sean Baumgart. 'Revealed: How Kevin Sheedy and GWS Got Their Man'. *Sydney Morning Herald*, 1 June 2010, 89.

Daffey, Paul. *Forward to Footy Town: Stories of Australia's Game*, edited by Paul Daffey and J. Harms, 1–2. Melbourne: Malarkey Press, 2013.

Daffey, Paul. *Local Rites*. Flemington: Black Duck, 2001.

Daffey, Paul. 'A Wonderful Tradition'. AFLVictoria, 6 May 2014, accessed 19 October 2015, http://www.aflvic.com.au/paul-daffey-wonderful-tradition/.

Das, Sourav. 'Top 10 Highest Paid Soccer Players 2015'. Sporteology, accessed 20 October 2015, http://sporteology.com/top-10-highest-paid-soccer-players-2015/.

Demetriou, Andrew. 'CEO's Report'. In *Australian Football League Annual Report 2013*, 21–32, accessed 6 March 2014, http://www.afl.com.au/staticfile/AFL%20Tenant/AFL/Files/Annual%20Report/2013%20AFL%20Annual%20Report.pdf.

Demetriou, Andrew. 'An Ongoing Challenge'. In *Australian Football League Annual Report 2005*, 24–29, accessed 5 August 2007, http://s.afl.com.au/staticfile/AFL%20Tenant/AFL/Files/afl_annual_report_2005.pdf.

Denham, Greg. 'Karmichael Hunt Turns His Back on NRL Offers to Extend His Time with the Suns'. *The Australian*, 6 March 2012, accessed 7 March 2012, http://www.theaustralian.com.au/sport/afl/karmichael-hunt-turns-his-back-on-nrl-offers-to-extend-his-time-at-the-suns/story-fnca0u4y-1226289858372.

Denham, Greg, and Patrick Smith. 'AFL's Great Money Divide May Finally Be Shrinking'. *The Australian*, 11 June 2015, accessed 23 June 2015, http://www.theaustralian.com.au/sport/afl/afls-great-money-divide-may-finally-be-shrinking/story-fnca0u4y-1227392144351?sv=ab12a4e68a19d4267206398519d0f72c.

Department of Economic Development, Tourism and the Arts. 'Bid Criteria'. Tasmania – It's Time, accessed 14 March 2013, http://www.tassiefootyteam.com.au/bid_criteria.php.

Department of Economic Development, Tourism and the Arts. 'A History of Football in Tasmania'. Tasmania – It's Time, accessed 31 March 2013, http://www.tassiefootyteam.com.au/history.php.

Department of Economic Development, Tourism and the Arts. 'Messages of Support'. Tasmania – It's Time, accessed 14 March 4, 2013, http://www.tassiefootyteam.com.au/your_support.php.

Department of Economic Development, Tourism and the Arts. '10 Reasons Tassie Should Have an AFL Team'. Tasmania – It's Time, accessed 31 March 2013, http://www.tassiefootyteam.com.au/ten_reasons.php.

Desbordes, Michel. *Marketing and Football: An International Perspective*. Amsterdam: Butterworth-Heineman, 2007.

Devaney, John. Carlton. In 'Australian Football: Celebrating the History of the Great Australian Game', AustralianFootball.com, accessed 28 March 8, 2011, http://australianfootball.com/clubs/bio/Carlton/3.

Devaney, John. Fitzroy. In 'Australian Football: Celebrating the History of the Great Australian Game', AustralianFootball.com, accessed 9 February 2013, http://australianfootball.com/clubs/stats/Fitzroy/31.

Devaney, John. North Melbourne. In 'Australian Football: Celebrating the History of the Great Australian Game', AustralianFootball.com, accessed 27 April 2013, http://australianfootball.com/clubs/stats/North%2BMelbourne/13.

Devaney, John. Sydney. In 'Australian Football: Celebrating the History of the Great Australian Game', AustralianFootball.com, accessed 9 February 2013, http://australianfootball.com/clubs/bio/Sydney/11.

Devaney, John. Western Bulldogs. In 'Australian Football: Celebrating the History of the Great Australian Game', AustralianFootball.com, accessed 27 April 2013, http://australianfootball.com/clubs/bio/Western%2BBulldogs/14.

Dillon, Andrew, and Clothier, Brett. 'Legal and Integrity', in *Australian Football League Annual Report 2015*, accessed 1 June 2016, http://s.afl.com.au/staticfile/AFL%20Tenant/AFL/Files/Annual%20Report/AFLAnnualReport2015.pdf.

Dowsing, Jeff. 'Era, Era on the Wall: 1949–1959'. Part 3 – Safe at Home, and Away. *The Footy Almanac*, accessed 22 October 2015, http://www.footyalmanac.com.au/era-era-on-the-wall-1949-1959/.

Duncan, Samuel. 'How the Play Element Has Changed in Australian Football and the Consequences of This Change on Community'. Unpublished doctoral thesis, Swinburne University of Technology, Hawthorn, Victoria, 2015.

Durkheim, Emile. *The Division of Labor in Society*. New York: Free Press, 1933.

Durkheim, Emile. *Suicide*. New York: Free Press, 1951.

East, Bernard. *Australian Rules Football in a Commercial Era – Catering for Theatregoers and Tribals*. Sydney: Walla Walla Press, 2012.

Elsworth, Sophie. 'Gary Ablett Jnr Signs Deal with Gold Coast Suns'. Courier Mail, 29 September 2010, accessed 29 September 2010, http://www.couriermail.com.au/sport/afl/gary-ablett-jr-lets-slip-imminent-announcement-of-deal-with-gold-coast-suns/story-e6frepf6-1225931171781

'English Premier League TV Deal: Sky and BR Outlay $10 Billion in Stunning Three-Season EPL Outlay'. Fox Sports Australia, 11 February 2015, accessed 11 February 2015, http://www.foxsports.com.au/football/premier-league/english-premier-league-tv-deal-sky-and-bt-outlay-10-billion-in-stunning-three-season-epl-outlay/story-e6frf4a3-1227215447239.

Essendon Football Club. 'Club History', Essendon, accessed 10 September 2012, http://www.essendonfc.com.au/our-club/history.

Essendon Football Club. 'Community', Essendon, accessed 1 June 2016, http://www.essendonfc.com.au/community.

Evans, Mark. 'Football Operations' in *Australian Football League Annual Report 2015*, accessed 1 June 2016, http://s.afl.com.au/staticfile/AFL%20Tenant/AFL/Files/Annual%20Report/AFLAnnualReport2015.pdf.

Fédération Internationale de Football Association (FIFA). Laws of the Game 2012/2013. Zurich: Author, n.d., accessed 1 May 2012, http://www.fifa.com/mm/document/footballdevelopment/refereeing/81/42/36/lawsofthegame_2012_e.pdf.

Fitzpatrick, Mike, and McLachlan, Gillon. 'Chairman and CEO's Reports,' in *Australian Football League Annual Report 2015*, accessed 1 June 2016, http://s.afl.com.au/staticfile/AFL%20Tenant/AFL/Files/Annual%20Report/AFLAnnualReport2015.pdf.

Flanagan, Martin. *The Call*. St. Leonards: Allan and Unwin, 1998.

Frank, Thomas. *One Market under God: Extreme Capitalism, Market Populism and the End of Economic Democracy*. London: Vintage, 2002.

'Free Agency', AFL.com, accessed 28 March 2013, http://www.afl.com/au/afl-hq/the-afl-explained/free-agency.

Frost, Lionel, Margaret Lightbody, and Abdel Halabi. 'Expanding Social Inclusion in Community Sport Organisations: Evidence from Rural Australian Football Clubs'. Discussion Paper 31/13, Monash University, Business and Economics, 2013, accessed 29 March 2015, http://business.monash.edu/economics/research/publications/2013/3113expandingfrostlightbodyhalabi.pdf.

'Full Statement from Essendon

Chairman David Evans', AFL.com, accessed 27 February 2013, http://www.afl.com.au/news/2013-02-27/full-statement-from-essendon.

'Full Statement from the AFL', AFL.com, accessed 5 May 2013, http://www.afl.com.au/news/2013-02-07/full-statement-from-the-afl.

'A Full Statement: Melbourne Tanking Penalties', AFL.com, accessed 28 March 2013, http://www.afl.com.au/news/2013-02-19/afl-full-statement-melbourne-tanking-penalties.

Gare, Arran. 'The Neo-Liberal Assault on Australian Universities and the Future of Democracy: The Philosophical Failure of a Nation'. Concrescence: *The Australasian Journal of Process Thought* 7 (2006): 21–41.

Goffman, Erving. *Interaction Ritual: Essays on Face to Face Behaviour*. Chicago: Aldine Transaction, 1967.

Goldlust, John. *Playing for Keeps: Sport, the Media and Society*. Melbourne: Longman Cheshire, 1987.

Grant, Trevor. 'Battle Grounds'. *Herald Sun*: 'Our Game: 150 Years of Footy', 5 May 2008, 20.

Grant, Trevor. 'The Reluctant Star'. *Herald Sun Weekend*, 22 April 2006, 10–11.

Green, Thomas Hill. 'Lecture on "Liberal Legislation and Freedom of Contract"'. In T. H. Green: *Lectures on the Principles of Political Obligation and Other Writings*, edited by Paul Harris and John Morrow, 195–212. Cambridge: Cambridge University Press, 1986.

Grigg, Angus. 'Gentleman's Code'. *The AFR Magazine*: Supplement of the Australian Financial Review (March 2006), 60–70.

Gunston, Ray. 'Financial Report', in *Australian Football League Annual Report 2015*, accessed 1 June 2016, http://s.afl.com.au/staticfile/AFL%20Tenant/AFL/Files/Annual%20Report/AFLAnnualReport2015.pdf.

Gusfield, Joseph. R. *The Community: A Critical Response*. New York: Harper Colophon Books, 1975.

Hans, J. S. *The play of the world*, University of Massachusetts Press, Boston, 1981

Hawthorn Football Club. Annual Financial Report: Year Ending 31 October 2007, accessed 15 October 2012, http://www.hawthornfc.com.au/staticfile/AFL%20Tenant/Hawthorn/PDFs/HFC_2007_Annual_Financial_Report.pdf.

Hawthorn Football Club. Hawthorn FC Membership, accessed 14 March 2013, http://membership.hawthornfc.com.au/2013-packages.

Hegel, Georg. *Philosophy of Right*. Vol. 46, Britannica Great Books of the Western World. London: Encyclopaedia Britannica, 1952.

Hegel, Georg. *Philosophy of Right*. Translated by T. M. Knox. London: Oxford University Press, 1967.

Herald Sun, 9 December 2011.

Hess, Robert. 'Women and Australian Rules Football in Colonial Melbourne'. *International Journal of History and Sport* 13, no. 3 (December 1996): 356–72.

Hess, Robert, and Bob Stewart (eds.). *More than a Game: An Unauthorised History of Australian Rules Football*. Melbourne: Melbourne University Press, 1998.

Hird, James. 'Home Is Where the Heart and Soul Is'. *Herald Sun*, 12 April 2006, 90.

Hirschi, Travis. *Causes of Delinquency*. Berkeley: University of California Press, 1969.

Hisgrove, Dorothy. 'People, Customer and Community Report'. In *Australian Football League Annual Report 2013*, accessed 6 March 2014, http://www.afl.com.au/staticfile/AFL%20Tenant/AFL/Files/Annual%20Report/2013%20AFL%20Annual%20Report.pdf.

'History of Windy Hill, Essendon'. Shawfactor, accessed 17 October 2012, http://www.shawfactor.com/reference/history-of-windy-hill-essendon.

Hocking, Jenny, and Nell Reidy, 'Marngrook, Tom Wills and the Continuing Denial of Indigenous History: On the Origins of Australian Football', *Meanjin*, 75, no. 2 (June 2016), https://meanjin.com.au/essays.marngrook-tom-wills-and-the-continuing-denial-of-indigenous-history

'How Much Does It Cost to Get an NRL and AFL Grand Final TV Advertising Spot?' Mumbrella, accessed 3 October 2015, http://mumbrella.com.au/how-much-does-it-cost-to-get-an-nrl-and-afl-grand-final-tv-advertising-spot-322414.

Hughes, A. 'The Jewish Community'. In *Sporting Immigrants: Sport and Ethnicity in Australia*, edited by Richard Cashman, Philip Mosely, John O'Hara, and Hilary Weatherburn, 103. Crows Nest: Walla Walla Press, 1997.

Huizinga, Johan *Homo Ludens: A Study of the Play-Element in Culture*. London: Routledge and Kegan Paul, 1949.

Huizinga, Johan. *Homo Ludens: A Study of the Play-Element in Culture*. Boston: Beacon Press, 1950. First published 1938 by Wolters-Noordhoff.

Huizinga, Johan. *Men and Ideas: History, the Middle Ages, the Renaissance: Essays by Johan Huizinga*. Trans. J. S. Holmes and H. V. Marle. New York: Harper and Row, 1970.

Hutchinson, Colin. 'How the Teams Got Their Names'. In *100 Years of Australian Football 1897–1996: The Complete Story of the AFL*, edited by John Ross, Ringwood: Viking, 1996.

Hutchison, Garrie, Rick Lang and John Ross. *Roar of the Lions, Fitzroy Remembered 1883–1996*. Melbourne: Lothian Books, 1997.

Klugman, Matthew. *Passion Play: Love, Hope and Heartbreak at the Footy*. Melbourne: Hunter Publishers, 2011

Irving, Helen. *To Constitute a Nation: A Cultural History of Australia's Constitution*. Cambridge: Cambridge University Press, 1999.

Jacobs, Jane. *The Death and Life of Great American Cities*. New York: Random House, 1993. First published 1961.

Joseph, Ron. 'North Melbourne Football Club Best and Fairest'. Speech given at North Story, the 80th Anniversary Gala held at the Royal Exhibition Centre, Melbourne, 18 March 2005, accessed 18 November 2009, http://en.academic.ru/dic.nsf/enwiki/13480.

Kanter, Rosabeth Moss. *Commitment and Community: Communes and Utopias in Sociological Perspective*. Cambridge, MA: Harvard University Press, 1972.

Lake, Marilyn. *Alfred Deakin's Dream of Independence*. Melbourne: Deakin University, 2006.

Lando, Lou. 'Israel Folau Is Doomed to Fail with GWS Giants'. Tenplay.com, 9 February 2012, accessed 9 February 2012, http://tensport.com.au/news /theroarAFL-Israel-Folau-is-doomed-to-fail-with-GWS-Giants.htm.

Lanigan, Roslyn. 'How Much Is Your Local Footy Team Worth?', *Weekly Times*, 26 March 2014, accessed 26 March 2014, http://www.weeklytimesnow.com.au/sport/how-much-is-your-local-footy-team-worth/story-fnkerdz1-1226864231606.

Lasch, Christopher. *The Culture of Narcissism: American Life in an Age of Diminishing Expectations*. London: Abacus, 1980.

Lethlean, Simon. 'Game and Market Development', in *Australian Football League Annual Report 2015*, accessed 1 June 2016, http://s.afl.com.au/staticfile/AFL%20Tenant/AFL/Files/Annual%20Report/AFLAnnualReport2015.pdf.

Lindsay, Margaret. 'Taking the Joke Too Far and Footballers' Shorts'. In *Gender, Sexuality and Sport: A Dangerous Mix*, edited by Dennis Hemphill and Caroline. Symonds, 61–67. Sydney: Walla Walla Press, 2002.

Main, Jim. *In the Blood: South Melbourne–Sydney Swans Football Club*. Bayswater: BAS, 2009.

Mancini, Anne, and Gillian M. Hibbins. *Running with the Ball: Football's Foster Father*. Melbourne: Lyndoch, 1987.

Maplestone, Michael. *Flying Higher: History of the Essendon Football Club 1872–1996*. Melbourne: Essendon Football Club, 1996.

Markoff, Barry. *The Road to 'A' Grade: A History of the Ajax Football Club*. Clayton South: Brownhall Printing, 1980.

McLachlan, Gillon. 'CEO's Report,' in *Australian Football League Annual Report 2015*, accessed 1 June 2016, http://s.afl.com.au/staticfile/AFL%20Tenant/AFL/Files/Annual%20Report/AFLAnnualReport2015.pdf.

Mclean, Brock. 'On the Couch: Interview with Brock Mclean'. Fox Footy, Fox Sports, 30 July 2012.

McMillan, David, and David Chavis. 'Sense of Community, a Definition and Theory'. *Journal of Community Psychology* 14, no. 1 (1986): 6–23.

Millar, Susanna. *The psychology of play*. Oxford: Penguin Books, 1968

Murdoch, Walter. *The Australian Citizen: An Elementary Account of Civic Rights and Duties*. Christchurch: Whitcombe and Tombs, 1926.

Murdoch, Walter. *Loose Leaves*. Melbourne: George Robertson, 1909.

Murray, Bill. *Introduction to Football: A History of the World Game*. Hampshire: Scolar Press, 1994, xiii–xiv.

'NAB Draft Hub', AFL.com, accessed 19 October 2015, http://www.afl.com.au/draft/draft-history.

'NAB Fantasy', AFL.com, accessed 11 June 2012, http://fantasy.afl.com.au/pulse/index.html#/pulse.

Nadel, Dave. 'The Professionalisation and Commercialisation of Australian Football, 1975–1996'. Doctoral thesis, Monash University, Melbourne, 2000.

Nadel, Dave. 'What is a Football Community?' in *Occasional Papers in Football Studies*, Vol. 1, No. 1, 1998.

Nicholson, Matthew. 'Print Media Representation of Crisis Events in Australian Football'. PhD thesis, Victoria University, 2002, accessed 27 March 2012, http://vuir.vu.edu.au/344/1/05chapter4.pdf.

'Nissan Super Coach,' *Herald Sun*, accessed 11 June 2012, http://supercoach.heraldsun.com.au.

North Melbourne Football Club. 'New Partner for North'. NMFC.com, 25 September 2011, accessed 14 March 2013, http://www.nmfc.com.au/news/2011-09-25/new-partner-for-north.

O'Loughlin, Heath. 'History: North in Hobart'. NMFC.com, accessed 16 October 2012, http://www.nmfc.com.au/news/2011-09-27/history-north-in-hobart.

O'Regan, Tom. 'The Rise and Fall of Entrepreneurial Television, 1986–92'. In *Australian Television Culture*, 40–59. St Leonards: Allen and Unwin, 1993.

Orive, Sasha. *Victorian Rules: Populi Ludus Populo – The Game of the People for the People*. Melbourne: State Library of Victoria, 1996

Pennings, Mark *Origins of Australian Football: Victoria's Early History: Volume 1: Amateur Heroes and the Rise of Clubs, 1858 to 1876*. Redland Bay: Connor Court Publishing, 2012.

Pusey, Michael. *Integrity under Stress: Economic Rationalism in Canberra – A Nation Building State Changes Its Mind*. Cambridge: C.U.P., 1991.

Putnam, Robert. 'Bowling Alone: America's Declining Social Capital'. *Journal of Democracy* 6, no. 1 (1995): 65–78.

Putnam, Robert. *Bowling Alone: The Collapse and Revival of American Community*. New York: Simon and Schuster, 2000.

Putnam, Robert. *Making Democracy Work: Civic Traditions in Modern Italy*. Princeton: Princeton University Press, 1993.

Ralph, Jon. 'No Looking Back'. *Herald Sun*, 29 February 2008, 106.

Reed, Ron. 'Swans Sparks but No Flair'. *The Herald*, 23 September 1981, 41.

Richardson, N. 'Saturday Night Replay: How the Sporting Globe Came to Change Australian Rules Football in Victoria during the 1920s'. *Sporting Traditions* 31, no. 1 (May 2014), 121.

Rickard, John. *An Assemblage of Decent Men and Women: A History of the Anglican Parish of St Mary's North Melbourne 1853–2000*. North Melbourne: St Mary's Anglican Church, 2008.

Riger, Stephanie, and Paul J. Lavrakas. 'Community Ties: Patterns of Attachment and Social Interaction in Urban Neighbourhoods'. *American Journal of Community Psychology* 9, no. 1 (1981): 55–66.

Rowe, David. 'Understanding Sport and Media: A Socio-Historical Approach'. In *Sport, Culture and the Media: The Unruly Trinity*, 2nd ed., 11–36. Berkshire: Open University Press, 2004.

Rudd, Kevin. 'The Global Financial Crisis'. *The Monthly*, 4 February 2009, accessed 15 January 2011, http://www.themonthly.com.au/tm/print/1421.

Sarason, Seymour. 'Commentary: The Emergence of a Conceptual Center'. *Journal of Community Psychology* 14 (1986): 405–7;

Sarason, Seymour. *The Psychological Sense of Community: Prospects for a Community Psychology*. San Francisco: Jossey-Bass, 1974.

Sawer, Marian. *The Ethical State? Social Liberalism in Australia*. Carlton: Melbourne University Press, 2003.

Sheahan, Mike. 'South Needs Compromise'. *Herald*, 7 October 1981, 52.

Slattery, Geoff. *The Australian Game of Football: Since 1858*. Docklands: Geoff Slattery Publishing, 2008.

Sleight, S. *Sponsorship: What It Is and How to Use It*. Berkshire: McGraw-Hill, 1989.

Smyth, Robert Brough. *The Aborigines of Victoria: With Notes Relating to the Habits of the Natives of Other Parts of Australia and Tasmania*. Melbourne: J. Ferres, Government Printer, 1878.

Spolin, Viola. *Improvisation for the Theatre*. 3rd ed. Chicago: Northwestern University Press, 1963.

'Sport: Touchstone of Australian Life'. *The Sport Factor*. Australian Broadcasting Corporation, 17 May 2001, accessed 11 June 2011, http://www.abc.net.au/radionational/programs/sportfactor/sport-the-touchstone-of-australian-life/3480856 (archived).

Steger, Manfred, and Ravi Roy. *Neoliberalism: A Very Short Introduction*. Oxford: Oxford University Press, 2010.

Stewart, Bob. *The Australian Football Business*. Kenthurst: Kangaroo Press, 1983.

Stewart, R. K. Introduction to 'The Economic Development of the Victorian Football League 1960–1984', n.d., accessed 9 February 2013, http://www.library/la84.org/SportsLibrary/SportingTraditions/1985/st0102/st0102c.pdf.

Styles, Aja. 'AFL Grand Final 2016 has highest footy ratings for Channel 7 in a decade'. *Sydney Morning Herald*, 2 October 2016, accessed 2 October 2016, http://www.srnh.corn.au/entertainrnent/tv-and radio/sport and-outdoors/afl-qrand-fl nal-2016-has-h 1qhest-footy-rat1nqs-forchannel-7-in-a-decade-20161002-grt3al.html.

Sutton-Smith, Brian. *The ambiguity of play*. Cambridge: Harvard University Press, 1997.

Taylor, Kevin. *The Sydney Swans: The Complete History, 1874–1986*. Sydney: Allen and Unwin, 1987.

Thompson, Matt, and Nathan Schmook, 'Essendon 34 appeal confirmed as players seek to clear their names', *AFL Media*, http://www.afl.com.au/news/2016-021-11/essendon-34-set-to-appeal-their-seasonlong-afl-bans, accessed 26/04/2016.

Tomlinson, Alan, and Christopher Young. *National Identity and Global Sport Events: Culture, Politics and Spectacle in the Olympics and the Football World*. Albany: State University of New York Press, 2006.

Tonnies, Ferdinand. *Community and Society*. Translated by C. Loomis. New York: Harper, 1957.

Tsakalotos, Euclid. 'Social Norms and Endogenous Preferences: The Political Economy of Market Expansion'. In *The Rise of the Market: Critical Essays* on the Political Economy of Neo-Liberalism, edited by P. Arestis and M. Sawyer, 5–37. Cheltenham: Edward Elgar, 2004.

United Nations Conference on Trade and Development. The Global Economic Crisis: Systemic Failures and Multilateral Remedies. New York: United Nations, 2009, accessed 15 March 2009, www.unctad.org/en/docs/gds20091_en.pdf.

Walsh, Brian. 'Corporate Affairs and Communications'. In *Australian Football League Annual Report 2010*, 63–65, accessed 17 January 2011, http://s.afl.com.au/staticfile/AFL%20Tenant/AFL/Files/afl_annual_report_2010.pdf.

Walsh, Brian. 'Growing Coverage Spreads Game's Appeal'. In *Australian Football League Annual Report 2010*, 63, accessed 16 March 2011, http://s.afl.com.au/staticfile/AFL%20Tenant/AFL/Files/afl_annual_report_2010.pdf.

Weston, James. *The Australian Game of Football*. Melbourne: Slattery Media Group, 2008.

Wilson, Caroline. 'Fair Call? No Way Say Clubs' Chief Executives'. *The Age Online*, 11 August 2006, accessed 11 August 2006, http://www.theage.com.au/afl//news/afl/fair-call-no-way-say-club-executives/200608/10/1154803032324.html.

Wilson, Caroline. 'Roos Fuming at Ten's Commentary'. *The Age*, 15 August, 2006, 89.

Wilson, Caroline, and Will Brodie. 'Footy's Favourite Son Rises to Gold Coast Challenge'. *The Age*, 29 September 2010, accessed 29 September 2010, http://www.theage.com.au/afl/afl-news/footys-favourite-son-rises-to-gold-coast-challenge-20100928-15w7u.html.

Wilson, William Julius. *The Truly Disadvantaged: The Inner City, the Underclass and Public Policy*. Chicago: University of Chicago Press, 1987.

Winnicot, Donald W. *Playing and Reality*. Penguin, Harmondsworth, 1974, 74.

World Anti-Doping Agency (WADA). *The 2013 Prohibited List: International Standard*. Author: 2012, accessed 28 March 2013, http://www.wada.ama.org/Documents/World_AntiDoping_Program/WADP-Prohibited-list/2013/WADA-Prohibited-List-2013-EN.pdf.

World Anti-Doping Agency (WADA). *The 2012 Prohibited List: International Standard*. Author: 2011, accessed 28 March 2013, https://wada-main-prod.s3.amazonaws.com/resources/files/WADA_Prohibited_List_2012_EN.pdf.

Appendix

AFL Fans Interviewed

Name	Club	Date of interview
Cheree Brown	Sydney	10 September 2015
Effie Caloutas	North Melbourne	1 September 2015
Neil Duncan	Geelong	15 May 2013
Alanna Ford	Carlton	8 September 2015
Josh Forte	Hawthorn	30 May 2013
Tom Gallimore	Brisbane	21 May 2013
Scott Hutchins	Geelong	22 May 2013
Zak Kardachi	Essendon	23 May 2013
Jason Lee	Essendon	13 June 2013
Stuart Osbourne	Essendon	20 May 2013
Jeremiah Ryan	Collingwood	6 June 2013
Michael Westland	Essendon	16 May, 2013
Phil Wild	Sydney	28 May 2013
Kate Withers	Geelong	31 August 2015

www.ingramcontent.com/pod-product-compliance
Lightning Source LLC
Chambersburg PA
CBHW071844080526
44589CB00012B/1109